TESTIMONIES From Emerson and

"Several times throughout the seminar my [...] and squeeze each other's hands when something you said really affected us. A couple times I looked over at him to make sure he was listening and he had tears in his eyes!"

"This is something that neither of us had heard before. It really affected how we both listened, interacted, and loved each other." J.E.

"The seminar... was unlike any I had heard before." P.T.

"I work with a woman who also went to the conference and she and I both agree that we learned a lot. What I want to know is, why doesn't anybody tell you this going in? ... if I knew then what I know now, I wonder how much of the tension and stress could have been avoided in my marriage."

"I can honestly say that seminar changed my life–our lives–forever…we were on the verge of divorce. As Christians, we both knew that this wasn't right and was not God's will for us but we seemed incapable of identifying our problems, let alone overcoming them. We just knew that things weren't working and had reached a dead end. ... The information that was pre- sented at the seminar was so simple and true, yet totally unknown to us and, I believe, the majority of all people."

"It was excellent to hear such a new approach. We always try to go to marriage retreats... But I don't think we really expected to hear anything new... Not this time! Your approach was perfect and so well grounded in scripture. ... I was glad for my spouse that his needs were being addressed and given a voice."

"I believe that your understanding of the nature of male emotional needs... is a real breakthrough. Your understanding of female emotional needs is no less accurate, but... has been... understood and taught." F.N.

"I feel like I have received a precious gift – the ability to better understand my husband's deepest needs. I always wanted to meet them, but did not understand how... My husband has always been a very quiet man – not one for displays of emotion. We are as different as any two people could be in that area. But, I see something so different in him as a result of this conference. He is as enthusiastic and excited as I have ever seen him." K.D

"Your knowledge of scripture and how to apply it was so helpful and encouraging. I heard things I had never considered before about my husband. He would attempt to let me know how he felt, but the words and spirit behind it never quite sunk in." C.S.

"I have used the concepts learned on the weekend in my practice. ...I had never really heard (this) emphasis... I think you really have it." J.B.

"God has certainly gifted you with the talent to speak to women about men and women. Thank you for touching our hearts." L.M.

"The whole weekend was like a second honeymoon. It was so interesting to us how biblically men and women are different." T.B.

"... over the course of 4 or 5 days... The difference was amazing. Our intimacy multiplied 400% in one week. He was like a different animal."

"Where would I even begin. I have not felt such peace in my life or in my marriage since courtship. I came to the conference reluctantly...at my husband's request." M.R.

"One gal... was saying that she would like to attend ONLY because...her husband needed to hear it... her husband cannot communicate! ... However, after you spoke...she said how much she learned...." D.A.

"Another thing that was enlightening about the seminar was why men clam up and walk away. I was one of those women who accused, "'You don't love me!'" NOW I see clearly." Female Missionary

"I believe my wife finally heard what I have been trying to tell her for the past 10 years. Your way of putting things in 'female terms' so she can understand is heaven-sent! Thank you very much. I also heard and better understand things about my wife – I thought it was just my wife, but I guess it is the way God made females (I've been known to say that I wish God made women to look like women but act like men!!)."

"As I sat there listening, I kept saying to my wife, 'That's how I feel. That's how I feel.'" Owner of two athletic clubs. B.O.

"(My husband) said how glad he was he had agreed to come. He said from all the books, tapes, counseling sessions, etc., he had read, listened to, talked about, etc…what you presented was the best material to date. I agree."

"The thing that impressed me the most was learning how men and women are wired differently. It is easier to understand what (my wife) is trying to get across to me. (My wife) and I will be celebrating our 33rd Anniversary... I WAS IMPRESSED!!!! J.W.

"No one else has ever shared with me the principles Dr. Eggerichs shares... He understands the intrinsic need men have and how important the fulfillment of this need is to marriage communication. My wife and I heard things that explained why we 'argue' the way we do and why we feel the way we feel, that were so accurate they seemed prophetic. I have never left a marriage seminar more excited and encouraged about my marriage." M.W.

"What an eye opener! I just sat there thinking, 'Yes! that's it!' We have studied the differences between the sexes before but your program nailed it, not only about what men & women need but how we retaliate when our needs aren't met. It has impacted how we've dealt with one another... it not only helped my wife & I understand each other better but it helped me understand myself better. I knew it in my heart but couldn't quite put my finger on it." J.W.

"I found your insight so relevant to us and our relationship and walked away with a greater understanding of each other, which at this time has been invaluable. We are still struggling through a difficult time... I believe you have tapped into something very profound." G.C.

Testimonies From An All-Women Workshop

"Will help save my marriage..."

"This is **a breakthrough for my marriage** & a prayer of my heart..."

"Life changing! ... Great! Very insightful... ******* (Can you give more stars???) Awesome!..."   "– I...saw light bulbs go off in my head..."

"**Deep**, WOW!! ... A way to share w/ my spouse. Terrific... Well done. Really hit home. So true!..."   "**Excellent**... It finally 'clicked' about my husband..."

"Awesome! New way of thinking – turned a light bulb on for me..."

"I really needed this. His was an answer to prayer. Great... Excellent! Love it! I learned a lot!"

"Thank you for giving us **a key to helping u**s build up our husbands..."

"What a great, great message!... It was awesome... Very helpful!..."

"Great to have a man's perspective. Mind blowing!... I appreciated the new information..."   "Awesome!... **I was inspired**... Very moving..."

"**Good insight** from Ephesians 5:33.... Very humorous and insightful. What an eye opener!..."

"Very helpful; easy to see; appreciated it much... Great!!... **Wonderful information!**..."

"Absolutely wonderful!... Helped me **understand how my husband thinks**. (Thanks)..."   "Wow – learned a lot... You may have just changed my marriage!..."

"**Convicting**, informative, **powerful**... Astounding!!..."

"10- Absolutely Awesome! ... Wow... **Total revelation**..."

"The **BEST marriage message** that I've ever heard! I plan to share this info w/ every married couple I know."

4

ABOUT Emerson and Sarah

As the senior pastor in a university town, Dr. Emerson Eggerichs had the privilege of studying the Bible thirty hours a week for nearly twenty years. And during that time in study he had the further privilege of making an absolutely extraordinary discovery about the secret of communication between husbands and wives. Using what he had learned in acquiring his Masters in Communication and his Ph.D. in Child and Family Ecology, Emerson crafted a unique message to share with couples everywhere who wish to improve their marriages. Emerson and Sarah have been married since 1973, and the principles they apply have worked powerfully in their own marriage. They long for you to experience what they've experienced.

Sarah Eggerichs, Emerson's wife, helped him shape the message from her perspective as a wife and mother. As the message slowly took shape they both became very excited at what they had to share – and with good reason. Both had endured troubling times from their families of origin, problems they had seen tear their families apart. Emerson's mother and father divorced when he was a year old, and then remarried each other. They separated again when he was five, and then once again came back together. The effect of this on him was profound. Sarah's family also has a widespread history of divorce. Given both their backgrounds, the idea that they might help others to overcome the difficulties of marriage has special significance to them.

Emerson and Sarah believe this message can make a gigantic difference in your marriage and family. And they are happy to invite you to join them as they discuss how to motivate your man God's way.

Emerson says, "As a pastor, I wept with wives in my office. Together, we struggled with ways to motivate their husbands to be more loving. I kept coming up with ways that she could be more loving. But, she was loving! And, when she loved him in different ways, it wasn't having the kind of impact we desired. One day it dawned on me to ask, 'What does the Bible say about motivating a husband to be more loving?' And I was a Bible teacher! What you hold in your hands is that discovery. This truth wipes away most of those tears."

Sarah says, "The last several years Emerson and I have been doing marriage conferences around the country. We have been sharing a message to which men are responding. I want to subtitle the Love and Respect Conference: 'The conference men want to attend!' Wives are asking their husbands, 'Is this the way you feel?' Men are saying, 'Absolutely.' And women ask, 'Why hasn't anybody told us this?' One wife said, "Your seminar supplied the 'missing piece' that made the information we already had click into place in a practical way." We believe there is one key word that could revolutionize your marriage. This is God's fundamental way to motivate husbands."

Emerson and Sarah Introduce The Secret

What husband – especially if he is a Christian – does not know that he is to love his wife? There are countless books on the subject, countless conferences and counseling programs. He's heard about it from radio and television programs. Generally speaking, husbands don't lack this knowledge. But what many of them do lack, for some reason, is motivation. If there's one thing we have discovered in our years in the pastorate counseling couples, it's that husbands really seem to lack motivation in this area! Boy oh boy, do they lack motivation! Who primarily seeks out marriage counseling? Who most often urges attendance at a marriage seminar? Who reads the books on marriage and leaves those books around to read? Who tries to get a spouse to change? You got it. She does. We felt that this was the fundamental problem in many of the marriage difficulties we encountered, and figuring out what to do about it has been the fundamental problem for marriage counselors all over. So what *does* motivate a husband to love, and feel more love for his wife? Why is this such a conundrum? Why isn't there a simple answer – and if there is a simple answer, why aren't people more aware of it?

Well, we did discover a simple answer. The only problem is that the simple answer we discovered is a huge secret. And how could it be anything but huge? After all, this is the secret that cracks the communication code between husbands and wives! It doesn't get much bigger than that! Maybe curing the common cold would come close... But why on earth should there be a secret about such a thing, something so fundamental to human experience? Why would something this important be so hard to discover? That's a story in and of itself. But the good news is that once you learn the secret – and it's a secret that *shouldn't* be a secret – you will be armed with something extraordinary. In reading the pages before you and putting into practice the principles we discuss, you will actually be able to effect positive changes in your marriage, probably to an extent about which you might only have dreamed before.

This isn't a speculative idea. We have both seen this work time and time again, and as you will see, it is profoundly biblical and profoundly simple. It *should* work! And we're happy to report that it does. It works for us. And this secret is powerfully simple, essentially nothing more than a single word. It's a word that is simple to learn. It will sound foreign to you at first, but it will be well worth mastering. That's because your husband thinks and speaks in this secret code, but you do not. And many times he's not even aware that he's speaking in code. But neither are you. In matters of intimacy, you, as a woman, think in terms of another code word. When these two words are not decoded, communication breaks down, messages get scrambled, and marriages get uncomfortable. So what is this code word that husbands speak in? Hang on! We'll get to that very soon!

But while we're on the subject, what is *your* secret code? Do you know? When you have a conflict, and you get especially upset and react negatively, it's usually because there is an issue deeper than the one you are arguing over. And when this deeper issue arises – whether you are aware of it or not – you instinctively react in a negative way. That negative reaction is you shouting to your husband in your code language. And you expect your husband to understand you. But he doesn't. He doesn't decode your code. So what is your code? In a nutshell, your code is, "I feel you are coming across *unlovingly*. Much too unlovingly." That's the *real* issue! Love!! That's your code!! As the Beatles sang, "All you need is love."

Love is the word that makes you tick, that animates so much else in your life, consciously and unconsciously. In the midst of an argument you might often think something like, "I am reacting to your failure to love me like I need to be loved. I expect you to *change* when I negatively react. I expect you to understand why I am negatively reacting. The code is obvious to me. You should decode the code! I feel love for you and want you to feel as much love for me. Please understand my need to be loved! Please change! Please act lovingly!"

But when you shout at him and he doesn't get it, what do you usually do? You shout *louder*. You are like the person talking to a foreigner who doesn't understand, so you say it again louder. But yelling doesn't help the foreigner translate. They don't need help with the volume of what you are saying; they need help with the meaning. They need a translation. They need to break the code. In matters of your love language, your husband is a foreigner. What will motivate him to decode the code? And, if he knows the basics of your love language, what will motivate him to be more loving in his reactions?

Motivating your husband has a lot to do with getting him to understand where you are really coming from – to get him to decode your secret code. So how do we get him to do that? What you are reading is all about that. It's about you energizing him and motivating him to understand your code. How? Well, we believe if you as a wife seek to understand your *husband's* code, he will seek to better understand *your* code. That's it. If you act on this, you will almost force him to act, to decode your code. That's part of what's so extraordinary and amazing about this! You will understand your husband *so that he might understand you*. And most extraordinary of all is that this actually works. We've seen it again and again. You must try to understand him in order to be understood yourself! It actually happens; be encouraged!

Let's think back for a moment. Have you recently had a conflict when you sensed the issue you were arguing about wasn't the *real* issue to your husband? We experienced this all the time early in our marriage, and we still do! In the course of the argument, did your husband's spirit suddenly and mysteriously deflate? Did it seem he was overreacting, even childish? Did he get angry and then withdraw? Did he react in a way that felt very unloving to you? Did he say something that was disrespectful? Okay, we're getting somewhere. (Your husband is like, me, Emerson!) What was happening was that your husband was speaking in his code! His message was obvious to him, but not to you! Just as your love language is obvious to you, but to him it's a foreign language. And just as it's upsetting to you when your husband doesn't understand *your* coded language, he cannot understand how you fail to hear what he is trying to communicate! That's because, like you, he speaks in his code language every day; though he's often unaware of it. And unfortunately for you – for both of you – he sends his coded message in negative, even childish, reactions that feel unloving to you. You don't see him speaking in code. You simply see him as being unloving! To you, he simply needs to be less angry and more understanding. So you keep negatively reacting, sending *your* coded message, hoping this will motivate him to change. And sadly, it doesn't!

So what can you do? As we have said and will say again and again

HER NEED FOR LOVE

If He Loved Me, He'd Figure This Out!

Okay, so Pink has a code. To Pink the code is clear: "If you love me as much as I love you, you'd figure out where I want to eat without me having to tell you."

But is Blue wrong? Pink did say, "I don't know, you decide." He could argue that she said she didn't know, but she did. She said, "you decide," but when he did, she decided against it. What's going on? In our experience, this sort of thing happens all the time.

We once spoke to a couple that had recently passed their tenth anniversary. There had been plenty of times over the last decade when the husband had forgotten their anniversary altogether. Usually his wife would drop hints, but he didn't seem to pick up on them. But when she said nothing he would miss it for sure. But this time, on their tenth wedding anniversary, somehow he remembered – and his wife hadn't said anything or even dropped any hints. He had gone to the drugstore and had looked at the cards on the rack, proud of himself that he was doing what he was doing and anticipating her reaction when he gave her the card. One card in particular on the rack immediately caught his eye. The colors, the words – it was absolutely perfect somehow. It was her. So he grabbed it, carried it to the counter, paid for it, and took his purchase home.

His wife was there when he arrived, so he took the card in the other room to sign it and hurriedly put it in the envelope. He wrote her name on the envelope, came out, and presented it to her, smiling. And sure enough, when he handed her the card, she beamed from ear to ear. She was so happy – he had finally remembered! After ten years! And so with great joy she opened the card and began to read it. Then her face fell. "What's wrong?" he asked, concerned.

"**...Like a wife forsaken and grieved in spirit...when she is rejected...**" - Isaiah 54:6

For a moment there was silence. Then she spoke. "It's a birthday card," she replied.

So where do you imagine this conversation went next? We can picture it pretty well.

"You're kidding," he exclaimed, grabbing for the card. "Unbelievable!"

"Yeah, unbelievable, all right," she says angrily.

"Well, hey – I made an honest mistake," he replied, bewildered. He knew he was full of good will; he had remembered their anniversary, and had bought her a card.

"You know," she said, "if you took your car in to be painted and they put a stripe on the side that was even a fraction of an inch off, you would have noticed that, right?" Now he is silent. She continues: "Because you care about that! But you don't care about this!"

He couldn't believe it. It wasn't fair. First she got angry and now she was moving on to character assassination? He started getting mad himself. "Hey, I made an honest mistake, all right? Give me a break!" He thought about her words some more, and how she had attacked him, and he got angrier. "You know what?" he said. "I'm glad I got you a birthday card!"

"**For that which I am doing, I do not understand; for I am not practicing what I would like to do, but I am doing the very thing I hate.**" - Romans 7:15

About a hundred and twenty seconds had passed. This couple, two people full of good will, had come home expecting to spend a wonderful, romantic evening together. Instead they ended up stomping to opposite ends of the house, staring out the window into the darkness. They were both dazed, wondering how they had gotten to this point, and thinking, "This is crazy. This is crazy."

Neither had decoded the code.

Men Have Two Brains...

Have you heard the expression that men have two brains...one of them is lost, and the other one is out looking for it? That's not very kind, but it's certainly the way men can seem to women sometimes.

Today, generally speaking, men know they are supposed to love their wives. What they tend to lack is the motivation to love them in ways that seem meaningful to the women. We believe this loss of motivation is because husbands and wives have conflicts, and these conflicts are the result of misunderstandings. Many husbands pull back because of a personal vulnerability within them as men – having to do with their code word. And when they pull back the wives feel very unloved.

Take this couple's conflict for example. Distressed over her excessive job responsibilities, upset over the broken garbage disposal, and anxious about getting a root canal at the dentist, a new wife says to her husband, "We need to talk."

As she pours out her frustrations about her job, he asks, "Did you talk to your boss about lightening the load?" When she talks about the disposal, he immediately says, "Sometimes bottle caps drop in there if you aren't careful." When she brings up the den-

> **"Then Elkanah her husband said to her, 'Hannah, why do you weep and why do you not eat and why is your heart sad? Am I not better to you than ten sons?'"**
>
> - I Samuel 1:8

tist, he immediately says, "Relax. The dentist will give you anesthesia before doing anything. You won't feel it a bit; I had it done a couple years back."

For each problem he offers a quick solution or helpful comment. But instead of making her feel better, he has only made her feel worse. She wanted sympathy and understanding, not solutions. "Why do you try to solve all my problems?" she yells. "Quit trying to fix me, and just listen to me! You men are all alike!"

In shock at her biting words, he goes silent. Here he was trying to help her! He leaves the house in anger and doesn't return for four hours. She can't believe he did that – she just doesn't understand it at all – and she cries herself to sleep. He has pulled back in a defensive reaction – and consequently she feels even *more* unloved. *Why* does this happen? *How* does this happen? God knows. That's not just an exasperated use of the phrase. God actually does know! And He's happy to share this knowledge with us. In fact, He *has* shared it with us. Again, that's what these pages are all about.

What's The Secret Code?

Have you ever been in a conflict where the issue is suddenly no longer the issue? We believe in the majority of those cases – when the issue isn't the issue – one thing is going on in the wife's heart and another thing is going on in her husband's heart. But why is this?

We believe it is the secret that cracks the communication code between male and female, between pink and blue. Here it is:

Beginning with you the wife, when the issue isn't the issue with you, we believe in the majority of the cases, the issue is simple: As wives, you most often react when feeling UNLOVED.

When the husband bought his wife an anniversary card that was actually a birthday card, the wife felt unloved. Her pink view of things concluded that if he loved her as much as she loved him, he would not make that kind of mistake. She became hurt and then angry. To him the issue was an honest mistake, but to her he was an unloving person.

"Does He Love Me As Much As I Love Him?"

One of the most common questions a wife asks herself is, "Does he love me as much as I love him?" Love is a woman's deepest need and value. This is why God's Word is so clear to husbands about love. She needs love and will wonder about it. The Bible commands the husband to love his wife with *agape* love. "Agape" love is God-like, unconditional love. No husband can do this perfectly, and he certainly can't do it in his own strength, nevertheless this is the kind of love that God commands husbands to have for their wives.

Scripture shows us that a wife needs this kind of love.

Ephesians 5:25   **Husbands, (agapao) your wives...**

Ephesians 5:28   **So husbands ought also to love (agapao) their own wives...**

Ephesians 5:33   **Nevertheless let each individual among you also love his own wife...**

Colossians 3:19   **Husbands, love your wives...**

Genesis 29:32   **And Leah conceived and bore a son... "now my husband will love me."**

Judges 14:16   **Samson's wife wept before him and said, "You only
                hate me, and you do not love me..."**
Judges 16:15   **Then she said to him, "How can you say, 'I
                love you,' when your heart is not with me?"**

Love is a wife's dominant need. Though Aretha Franklin sang the song "R.E.S.P.E.C.T." have you ever seen a greeting card from a husband to a wife that says, "Baby, I really respect you"? She doesn't want that card from her husband any more than she wants a tackle box and a subscription to *Field & Stream*. She wants to hear, "I love you." Of course every woman wants respect, too, but love is the bigger issue, the bigger need. Love, not R.E.S.P.E.C.T., is her dominant desire. And without love, a wife reacts negatively.

> "So husbands ought also to love their own wives as their own bodies. He who loves his own wife loves himself; for no one ever hated his own flesh, but nourishes and cherishes it, just as Christ also does the church." - Ephesians 5:28, 29

I, Emerson, can tell you story after story of times I came across as unloving to Sarah. Of course I'd much rather not. But for the purposes of getting our point across, let me give you one example. Okay, maybe two examples. The first one happened when I was in the middle of writing a book. We traveled to Santa Barbara visiting two of our children at college, and one morning I planned to sit down and write for a couple of hours. It was very clear in my mind that this was what I wanted to do. Then Sarah said to me, "I propose one of three things for us to do this morning..." I immediately gave her a distinctly negative look. You know, the "my plans are about to be interrupted and I am not happy" look. "You've got that look on your face," she said. The room got tense. My harsh look continued. Finally she said, "Oh, never mind." After a few more minutes of tension I spoke. "Okay," I said, "What are the three proposals?" (In years past when I wasn't writing a book on love, I might have gone several hours before softening.)

Hesitantly, she answered. "One, we can walk to that bagel shop and get a bagel. Two, we can drive there and get back quicker. Or, three, we can stay here, and you can write."

Obviously, Sarah was conscious of my desire to write. Her third proposal revealed that. I had wrongly presumed that she hadn't been conscious of that desire. I was an unloving person because I was trying to be a mind reader. The Bible says, "**Through presumption comes nothing but strife.**" (Proverbs 13:10). Too often my insolence and pride – the "I know what is going on here and I am right" attitude – would ignite an argument. When I gave her that negative look, Sarah felt devalued and unloved – and she was right. Through the years I cannot count the times that I came across this way. I grew up in a home where my dad would often explode in anger. I made a commitment not to do that. My mother rarely cried, but there were times she sobbed or got in the car and left. Women are not designed by God to be around harshness. When I am unkind and simmering with anger directed at Sarah, suddenly the issue is no longer the issue. The issue now is that she cannot believe I would talk that way – that is not love to her.

Another time, Sarah went to the grocery store to pick up some of my favorite foods. In return, she asked me if I would do the dishes, and I said I would. When she came home, the dishes were still undone. I had every intention of doing them, but I hadn't gotten to it by the time she returned. Sarah felt hurt. She cares about me and probably wouldn't do that if I asked her. So my action – or should I say my lack of action – came across as unloving to her.

These are not big, embarrassing examples, but they are only two from a long list. Sarah and I know that she needs to feel my love. We've been married since 1973. Time and time again I have failed to be loving in small ways like these two previous examples. Other times I have felt anger over things that weren't worthy of anger. This, too, has hurt her. Many times Sarah has asked me to show her love in small ways, but I somehow felt bothered and shrugged them off.

> "...now the man's name was Nabal, and his wife's name was Abigail. And the woman was intelligent and beautiful in appearance, but the man was harsh...in his dealings." - I Samuel 25:3

How many times have I come downstairs with the wrong shirt, and she sends me back upstairs? She is caring, but I feel annoyed. Or, how many times has she asked me to call so and so, since as a pastor I ought to do that kind of thing, yet I was irked that she was reminding me? How many times have I been irritated with the children when there was no just reason for being upset – they were being childish because they were children? Of course, as a man, I felt that I was being criticized for who I was. I sought to define what was going on and defend myself, and then ended up placing blame on her or somebody else. But then Sarah was hurt and felt unloved.

When the Issue Isn't the Issue

> "Put me like a seal over your heart, Like a seal on your arm. For love is as strong as death."
> - Song of Solomon 8:6

I have discovered that when the issue with Sarah is not the issue, usually she is feeling unloved or that I am coming across in an unloving manner. I've also learned that Sarah is most energized when I love her for who she is. She wants me to love her in ways that energize her. She knows she'll out love me if I do. Her problem, of course, is that I do not seem to love her like she loves me. So, naturally, she seeks ways to motivate me to love her like she loves me.

MOTIVATING A Husband

What Motivates A Husband To Love?

So we've covered how men and women speak different languages –
but what motivates a husband to love? Well, the

> **"and let us consider
> how to stimulate one
> another to love..."**
> - Hebrews 10:25

best way to get into that subject would be to talk
for a moment about what does *not* motivate him.
And even before that, let's take a look at what
unmotivates *you*.

For example, what would happen if someone asked your husband how
he felt about you and his reply was, "You know... I really... respect her."
Imagine if that person prodded him more specifically and asked, "Do you
love her?" and his response was, "Well... not really." How would you
feel? Of course you would be devastated, and rightfully so. If your husband said something like that, it could take you an awfully long time to get
over it, and many wives would never get over it. We've asked this question of hundreds of women and invariably get the same response: they
would be shattered and it would take forever to recover.

That's because between love and respect, love is by far a wife's greater
need. A wife needs love in the way that we all need air to breathe. And
wives want to be loved unconditionally. Even if you are unlovable, you
expect your husband to love you. In fact, if your husband doesn't love you
when you are especially unlovable, you feel that his behavior is especially
unloving. After all, if you have to earn his love, it isn't really love! If you
feel you have to earn his love, you shut down. You close off your spirit
from him. But when you are loved unconditionally – loved for who you
are – you are energized and motivated. Isn't that the case?

Now let's flip things around. What if you said of your husband, "You
know... I really love him... but respect? Many times I feel no respect for

29

him. I don't respect who he is. He doesn't deserve any respect." Do you know what he would feel if he heard you say that? Exactly. He'd be just as devastated as you would be if you heard him say he didn't love you. That's because a man needs respect like he needs air to breathe. The beautiful thing is that just as his love for you energizes you toward him, your respect – even when it's tough to give – energizes his desire to love you, not dominate you. We know you may not believe this, but it's true, as we shall see. In fact, it's the scriptural truth.

The bottom line is this: when a husband feels disrespected, he feels the message from his wife is, "I don't accept you for who you are as a man. I don't approve of who you are as a husband. And, I don't respect who you are as a human being." This shuts a man down. He closes off his spirit. On the other hand, when a wife feels unloved, she too feels unaccepted, disapproved and unloved for who she is as a person. Her spirit is wounded. This is the pink vs. blue dilemma. But, we've become a love-dominated culture. Most wives have little idea the depth of painful feelings men have when disrespected. Men don't display a crushed countenance and begin to cry. Instead, they get angry, go silent and withdraw. Or they attack with words of disrespect, seeking to equalize things. This goes over the heads of most wives. Instead, these women feel even more unloved.

The Secret That Cracks the Code

Did you know that according to the Bible, a husband's deepest need is for respect, not love? Said another way, during conflict, he needs to feel a wife's respect unlike any other thing. That's something that ought to get your attention if you haven't heard it before – and we're guessing you haven't. Did you know that in the Bible, wives are not commanded to agape/love their husbands? As we explained earlier, "agape" is the Greek word for God-like unconditional love. Instead, the apostles Paul and Peter instructed wives to show something else entirely. Each one of them concluded his teaching on marriage with an exhortation for wives to respect their husbands. Here are

> "we also speak, not in words taught by human wisdom, but in those taught by the Spirit, combining spiritual thoughts with spiritual words."
> - I Corinthians 2:13

the Scriptures we're talking about:

Ephesians 5:33   **Nevertheless let each individual among you also love his own wife even as himself; and let the wife see to it that she *respect her husband.***

1 Peter 3:1, 2   **your... husbands ...even if any of them are disobedient to the word, they may be won without a word by the behavior of their wives, as they observe your... *respect-ful behavior.***

Have you ever noticed this before? Have you ever even heard anyone speak of Paul's words and Peter's words on this subject? One woman we know, who co-chaired the National Day of Prayer, said to us, "I've read Ephesians 5:33 hundreds of times, but I never saw the word 'respect'." Hundreds of times and she never saw it.

What is respect? Scripture assumes every wife knows since no definition is given in each biblical text. For now, a better question is, what is disrespect? When a wife feels unloved, she can react in very negative ways that come across to a husband as disrespectful. Her tone, look, words and actions feel disrespectful to him. Added to that, many wives will say, "That's true. I don't feel any respect for him at those times. He doesn't deserve any respect. I love him but don't feel much respect. In fact, my disrespect should be a wake-up call to him. He needs to change." So, if wives don't know what respect is, they certainly know what disrespect is. They may not feel respect, but they certainly feel disrespect. We'll go deeper into this later.

Now, without question, a husband wants love, just as a wife wants respect. All of us need *both* these things. A husband especially yearns for love prior to meeting a woman, and during courtship. But the fact is, once into the marriage, husbands rarely ask, "Does she love me as much as I love her?" A husband almost always has a deep confidence that his wife loves him. His wife loves to love and he knows this. We might say that his love need is met. As we have said, ask a husband, "Does your

> "How beautiful is your love, my sister, my bride! How much better is your love than mine."
> - Song of Solomon 4:10

wife love you?" and the husband will usually say, "Yes." But if you ask him, "Does she like you?" he is apt to say, "No." Here's the secret. When in a conflict with your husband, and you sense the issue isn't the issue, in all probability he is feeling disrespected. He negatively reacts to you because he feels disrespected, not because he feels unloved. If that disrespect remains constant, he begins to lose motivation to move toward you with fond feelings of love. So, God's words – through Peter and Paul – are intended to guard a wife against being disrespectful. God knows that this horribly decreases the feeling of love in the marriage, so through Peter and Paul, God means to guide wives into the path of behavior that will increase her husband's feelings of love! I don't know about you, but I find that amazing. As one country preacher used to say, "Ain't God good?" And Victor Hugo said, "Nothing in the world is so powerful as an idea whose time has come."

Have you noticed that though a wife wants respect, if a husband is continually disrespectful she finally exclaims, "You don't even love me"? Her ultimate value is love. On the other side, though a husband needs love, if a wife is continually disrespectful, he finally exclaims, "I don't deserve this disrespect. Everybody respects me but you." His ultimate value is respect – at least when there is conflict. He is assured of her love in conflict, but not her respect. When he negatively reacts it is NOT to the feeling that she is an unloving person. He knows she is a loving woman. He is reacting to what appears to be, and in fact may be, her negative, disrespectful attitudes and actions. This can range from a cold stare to hands on the hips, or from yelling to throwing things. Rarely does he doubt her love. This is why when a wife puts on respect, something extraordinary can happen. When she discovers this one word and applies it, he is energized to love her.

One Husband Started Feeling Fond Feelings of Love!

A wife who is a nurse and married to a medical doctor e-mailed us their success story of when she decided to proactively act on her husband's need for respect: "I attended your marriage conference," she wrote. "I spoke with you briefly after the Friday night session and told you that my husband had filed for a divorce but was giving me some mixed signals about possibly getting back together some day. I had asked him to come to the conference with me and he had refused. You had suggested to me that I see if he would

> "'For I hate divorce,' says the Lord, the God of Israel.'" - Malachi 2:16

listen to the tapes. Before I even brought it up, he knew that I had purchased the tapes and he asked to listen to them. The divorce was in the final stages and he assured me that it would be finalized. From the very beginning I had many people praying for the restoration of our marriage and I continued to trust that if it was going to happen it would only occur with God's intervention. I don't know if it was the tapes or a combination of things but after that he began to draw closer to me and told me that he wanted to be a part of the family. ...(He) called his attorney and called off the divorce. (Then) he moved back home. We have been married for twenty years and our marriage is stronger now than it has ever been. …Respect was a huge issue in the eyes of my husband and one of the main reasons that he left. Once I saw how important it was to our entire relationship, it made it so easy for me to give my husband what he so desperately needed. The more I made him feel respected, the more he realized how much he loved me. We both had to go through many changes to get to the point that we are at today, but I thank the Lord for making me walk through the fire and the trials that I went through in order to make my marriage what it should be. We still have a lot of healing to do, but we are doing great and able to communicate with each other like never before. I just wanted to let you know how God had worked in our lives and thank you for your ministry."

Later, she e-mailed us again: "I really feel that God can use our relationship to help others and to encourage them. I continue to feel that everything that we went through was not only to help us but to help others too. As I was doing my devotions the other day I read II Corinthians 1:3,4: "...the Father of compassion and the God of all comfort, who comforts us in all our troubles, so that we can comfort those in any trouble with the comfort we ourselves have received from God." I really feel that God is going to use our troubles in some way to comfort others. Everything is still going amazingly well with us. My husband just told me yesterday that he never dreamed of feeling so in love with me and so content with our relationship. He said that he could have never felt this way with anyone but me and he is so glad that he is home and with his family. He also told me what a spiritual inspiration I have been to him and thanked me for not giving up on him. We never miss a night of praying together before we go to bed. I just thank God every day for what we have and hope that others can too find the healing in their home as we have. Thanks again for everything."

Then a third e-mail came: "Last week I had lunch with a friend and we got into an interesting topic about husbands. She wanted to know how we had worked things out and what had made the difference. She told me about some of the struggles she was having in her own marriage. Most of them again were respect kind of issues. I talked to her about some of the ways that we can come across to our husbands disrespectfully and why it is so hurtful to them. She was very excited about some of the things that I said to her and also asked to listen to your tapes. She said at the end of lunch that it had been the most enlightening lunch she had ever had. When I told her about (my husband) and I, she stated I thought maybe God might have something to do with it. I do not think that she is a Christian.

"The thing that was so encouraging to me is that years ago I would have just sat and listened to her and told how I agreed that her husband was wrong and how could he say the things that he did and then gone on to say negative things about my husband. I also was NEVER able to share with anyone that I was a Christian. It felt so good to uplift my marriage and my relationship with God and not be afraid to do so. I love being able to share that with others now and hope that God's love can really work through me. I also wanted to share with you that (my husband) and I continue to flourish. I am also seeing (my husband) become stronger and stronger in his relationship with Christ. We still do not miss a night of praying together and that has really helped to make a bond between us. We have come across a few situations that could have ended in hard feelings but we always seem to be able to talk it out and end up closer than before. Our love for each other seems to grow every day. It is so exciting to be so in love with him and to respect him so much."

Isn't this thrilling? Have confidence that this will happen to you. God is taking you into His Word. He is showing you that He does not command you to "agape-love" your husband but instead to show unconditional respect. You are less natural at reacting with respect and honor, so the Lord is protecting you by revealing to you a counter-move, so to speak, to your tendency to be disrespectful when feeling unloved. These pages will show you how to do this. For now, be encouraged that when you do this, fond feelings of love can return to a good-willed husband.

Now, before we move forward here, let's be clear on one thing. We are not arguing that you intend to be disrespectful or that he is correct in feeling you are disrespectful. We are just saying this is *how* he feels – when you sense the issue isn't the issue. When you see his spirit deflate or get provoked, in all probability he is looking through his respect lenses. He filters things this way. We are describing and explaining his feelings. For some mysterious reason, God made men this way. This is not to say He made men to react negatively, but He made them in such a way that, in their fallenness, they are prone to react negatively because they're especially sensitive in this one area, just as women are especially sensitive to feeling unloved. God's word confirms this dichotomy between the sexes.

And so the question before every wife is simple. Will she seek ways to invalidate her husband's feelings because in her opinion those feelings are uninviting, unacceptable and arrogant? Or, will she see this as God's revelation and gift to her to increase the feelings of love in their marriage?

This is no small teaching. Peter indicated that a wife's respectful behavior can win a disobedient man to God! He said it quite explicitly in 1 Peter 3:1, 2. And of course, if respectful behavior can win a disobedient husband to God, then it can also win that same husband back to his wife. That's because unconditional respect ignites something deep within the spirit of a husband. There is a profound and powerful reality here, and

> "For whatever was written in earlier times was written for our instruction, that through perseverance and the encouragement of the Scriptures we might have hope." - Romans 15:4

there is a mystery as well. As a woman, you know how hard it is for a wife to resist the unconditional love of a man. Her nature is designed to respond. What is left untaught today is that this is how husbands respond to unconditional respect. But because women don't feel this way, and instead feel this respect stuff points toward a man's haughtiness, they tend to dismiss or denounce this truth. Even for women who are open, their comment is, "This is so foreign." Even so, if one wants to travel Europe, learning a few vocabulary words goes a long way! A prudent wife learns one word. She refocuses on what God reveals about the nature of her husband. It is well worth the effort.

> **"...a prudent wife..."**
> - Proverbs 19:14

Yet, we hear the following sentiments hundreds of times. "I don't feel respect for him, not when he fails to love me. The problem in our marriage is his failure to love, not my disrespectful reactions. He causes my disrespectful reactions when he is unloving. On top of all of this, love is far more important than respect. Love is pure. Respecting a man is all about his ego. Yes, I admit I could be more respectful but sometimes only my disrespect motivates him to open up to me."

Even though the case has been made biblically and rationally, that a husband is won via unconditional respect, a wife can suddenly be overcome by hurt, frustration and anger. Emotions can take over. There is no way she is going to show respect when she doesn't feel respect. Because of some of the ideas of contemporary feminism, and because of her powerful emotions, this respect stuff doesn't "feel" right to her. So she lets herself get turned off. "He may be motivated by respect, but I am not motivated to show respect! No way! If I am going to feel any feelings of respect, it will be after he cherishes me. Then I'll be motivated! Since he has not done this, he is to blame for my disrespectful sentiments. This is his just due. He should be motivated to love me as I love him. He's at fault, not me. He isn't affectionate because he has a character flaw. You can't respect someone who isn't worthy of respect. You'd be respecting evil, and God isn't commanding me to respect wrongdoing!"

But again, a wife can fail to miss the point of Scripture and miss it in a colossal way. It isn't about him deserving respect but about her being a respectful, dignified woman in reaction to what she perceives to be his failure to love as he ought. As he is to be a loving man regardless of her performance, she is to be a respectful human being – no matter who she relates to. What is happening today is that some women have failed to learn the discipline of dignity independent of circumstances. As a result, when hurt, they are overcome by feelings of disrespect and even disdain. Biblically, this is sin. Her response is her responsibility. Her husband does not cause her to be a disrespectful human being. The amazing thing is that this needs to be heard again and again by some wives. We just talked to a wife who has heard the love and respect message several times. For the first time it dawned on her that her disrespectful attitude and failure to be a respectful human being had very little to do with her husband! In the area of intimacy, a husband is not as natural at loving, just as a wife is not as natural at respecting. In our culture, though, we condemn the husband as an unloving human being when he is unloving, but when a wife is disrespectful, we blame the husband again. This is not of God. This is not biblical. Michal, King David's wife, despised David in her heart. This was her issue, not his.

King David Needed What His Wife Wouldn't Give Him

"Then it happened as the ark of the Lord came into the city of David that Michal the daughter of Saul looked out of the window and saw King David leaping and dancing before the Lord; and she despised him in her heart" (2 Samuel 6:16).

"But when David returned to bless his household, Michal the daughter of Saul came out to meet David and said, "How the king of Israel distinguished himself today! He uncovered himself today in the eyes of his servants' maids as one of the foolish ones shamelessly uncovers himself!" (2 Samuel 6:20).

God's Word tells us that Michal was wrong to have such disdain. David had good intentions, but she scorned him – and we see how he recoiled at her disrespectfulness! "And I (David) will be more lightly esteemed than this...I will be distinguished. And Michal the daughter of Saul had no child to the day of her death" (2 Samuel 6:22,23).

Was David arrogant for wanting to be esteemed? Too many women miss what men mean when they say these things. Just as men can miss what women are saying when they declare, "I just want somebody to love me. I want to be the object of someone's love. I want to be special." Many men don't get this heart cry at all, thinking a woman is clinically egotistical or just plum loco. But what man in his right mind would say such a thing? He's been taught that such feelings in women are legitimate. This is a need, not some self-serving desire. But the same thing was true of David's feelings. He needed to be honored, respected and esteemed for who he was as a human being. He was vulnerable to Michal's disdain for him. God did not design husbands to be married to women full of contempt. But he also did not design men to cry in the face of contempt, which is unfortunate because the inner pain goes unnoticed. Michal was wrong for concluding David was unacceptable; flat out wrong, and in sin. At that moment though, she may have been the last to see it. Further, what is sad is that wives do not see themselves as being that powerful when showing contempt. To most wives, it is rooted in a desire to get some positive message across. Michal may have felt she was mothering David. Many women simply do not grasp men's vulnerability to contempt or the appearance of contempt. It is comparable to a husband's harshness with a wife. The difference, of course, is that women cry and men get angry. So women come out looking vulnerable and men looking unloving.

Again, we observe the love and respect connection. When Michal despised David, it did not ignite fond feelings of love in his heart for her. The marriage ended. One wonders if Michal ever saw the sin of her disdain, or if she held onto her view as the righteous position.

We believe that men need to be honored as honorable men. David needed to be esteemed. David was not an egotist. He was simply not designed by God to be spoken to in this fashion. Her disdain ripped his heart. She saw him as strong. In her mind, he should be able to take it, but Michal, along with many wives, are clueless at the vulnerability of the male spirit to such disrespect. Even King David, as a man, was overwhelmed by that condescension and dishonor.

"Well," a wife may argue, "if what you say is true, then why does my husband not complain about my disrespect like I complain about his lack of love?" He may have but you didn't hear it. Over time, he's grown silent. If you will recall, you may have said, in all honesty, "I don't feel any respect for you at times like that." This equals him saying, "I don't love you at times like that." If he said that though, you'd be up in arms; love is to be unconditional. As for respect, in this culture, what can he say to you? You believe he must fulfill conditions to be respected. So, he goes silent on that topic. In fact, he thinks respect must be earned, too, but he shouts, "I don't deserve this kind of disrespect." Some men have also learned that complaining results in several hours of talking with you to clear the air. All that will come of this is your belief that he is at fault for your negative response. You are hurt, and he is insensitive. That is not energizing to a husband. If every conversation ends with it being pointed out that he is unloving and thus not deserving of admiration, what is the point in going there? He does not feel the need to bring the relationship up to date emotionally when this is the sum of things. It is easier to drop it, forget it and move on. This is less exhausting to him. Would you be excited if at the end of every marital dialogue it was pointed out to you that you were disrespectful and needed to earn love?

Recently a wife told us, "My husband doesn't complain about me, but I complain about him all the time. This proves in my view that I am better, and he is the problem." First of all, she could be correct to a certain point. Maybe her husband does have problems. Maybe she is a woman of dignity and respect. Maybe she is a quality woman. On the other hand, she may be married to a man who is far more loving toward her than she is respectful toward him. In other words, he is obeying God's command to love her far more than she is obeying God's command to respect him. What she does not see, of course, is that she is designed by God to be more natural at loving in ways that are meaningful to her than he is at loving in ways that are meaningful to her. So, she scores high on the love scale and he scores low. And, because being a respectful person during a fight does not show up on her marital score card, she isn't failing. Because respect is not part of her criteria for judging the quality of her personhood and love is, she comes out as the better person.

As for him not complaining, generally women complain and criticize, whereas men get defensive and withdraw. Because a man is not venting does this mean he is worse than her? No. It may simply mean he is an honorable man who does not complain and criticize. He deals with his hurts by sucking them up. Not wrong, just different. Solomon said, "A fool's vexation is known at once, but a prudent man conceals dishonor" (Proverbs 12:16). We wonder if the truth in many evangelical homes is that the wives are the fools and the husbands are prudent. You won't hear that preached. It doesn't sell merchandise. Remember, too, that when a wife gets hurt, eventually, most wives will cry. She can sob and sob. Oh, how we ignore the obvious sometimes. Yet, this speaks volumes. We see her vulnerability in her weeping. Few men ever cry. They don't want to cry. When disrespected, they get angry and this puts them in a bad light. Even if they go silent without anger, this is condemned. On top of that, when a wife gets angry, she expects her husband to understand her deeper hurt. When he gets angry, she expects her husband to change. He is hurting her.

We need to evaluate marriage differently. We need the love scale BUT ALSO a respect scale. For example, on the love scale, between one and ten, he scores a 6 and she scores a 9.5. On the respect scale, he scores an 8.5 and she scores a 5. On total, he is 14.5 of 20. She is 14.5 of 20. In God's eyes, the husband and wife are equal, and on average, doing okay! But today, since love is the dominating criteria in our culture for passing judgment on marriage, he is flunking at 65% and she is getting an A at 95%. Is this why so many wives confess that they are so judgmental toward their husbands? Have they been conditioned to see the marriage through pink lenses, which color in a very bad light what they see in their husbands? Does this explain why so many women acknowledge that they feel they are the better sex, why they complain, and why they admit, "I have to stop being my husband's holy spirit?" If pink lenses were the only lenses through which life was to be seen, then yes, women would be better. But God's Word reveals He made them male and female, and His Word adds a wife's respect toward her husband as a criteria equal to a husband's love for his wife. We need to return to the standard of measure established in God's Word. This is not to shame any woman but to help her appreciate the man God has given her, value the truth of God's word, and get in tune with the power of respect.

Today, 2 to 1 and maybe 3 to 1, wives are initiating divorce. Many men will stay in the marriage. For all we hear about men's lack of commitment, many are committed. The men are not as interested in bailing out. Yes, yes, we know the line from some wives. "I am unhappy. My needs aren't being met." That though, is pink speaking as she looks at the marriage through the love lenses. She feels less love from him than she gives, so finally wears out and calls it quits. How sad that she did not treasure the power of respect talk as a way of motivating him to be more loving and discover what her disrespect was doing to de-motivate his love.

If the truth were known, your husband might conceivably be seeking to love you more than you are seeking to be respectful. Elkanah was married to Hannah. The Bible says, "he loved Hannah" (1 Samuel 1:5). Yet, during a very distressful time in Hannah's life when she could have no children, Elkanah tried to comfort her. He was solution-oriented. He tried to solve her problem by asking, "Hannah, why do you weep and why do you not eat and why is your heart sad? Am I not better to you than ten sons?" (1 Samuel 1:8). Today's woman might blast that phrase, "Am I not better to you than ten sons?" To some wives, that proves the man is clueless on how to love, and further, that he is an egotist. It is all about him. He has no empathy. Yet, the Bible says, "he loved Hannah." Is God calling you to trust Him on what He says is going on inside your husband? Is it possible that your husband is more loving than you think, and is only reacting unlovingly because he feels disrespected? Be open to this. And step out in faith. When you

"Wives...to your own husbands, as to the Lord." - Ephesians 5:22

"...precious in the sight of God." - I Peter 3:4

do this toward a good-willed husband, it works. Even though you are not motivated by respect, you are motivated by your love for God. If for nothing more, show unconditional respect because you love God and His Word.

How Male Leaders Motivate Men To Serve and Die

I, Emerson, went to a military academy and had plenty of opportunity to observe how men motivate one another, how they relate to each other, and what makes an effective leader. Leaders are effective when they treat their men with honor and respect. Unconditional respect for a man and confidence in who he is comes first, even if his performance is not there.

Men do two things in the military when respected for who they are as men. First, they serve. That's why men called it the "service." Second, they die; they give their lives in defense of their ideals. Oh, that you would hear this all-important message! Men serve and die! Please realize how

"be men...be men and fight." - I Samuel 4:9

powerful this unconditional honor toward men is. Consequently, when husbands are respected, they do not treat their wives in subservient ways but serve them. Men do not "kill" women emotionally, but die for them. This is true for every husband who has basic good will.

When your husband became attracted to you, it was because of the look of admiration in your spirit and in your eyes when he walked into the room. That look made him feel he could take on the world. Because of that look he made a decision to serve you, and even die. One husband said, "I love you so much, I'd die for you." His wife said, "Oh, Harry, you keep saying that but you never do."

Seriously, do you want to try to speak this one word? In courtship you used that word and communicated that attitude. Are you interested in tasting again the power of what we're discussing? What is different now, though, is that you can have a better understanding of what best motivates your husband. In courtship, you thought it was your love that motivated him. After all, love motivates you. He should feel the same way! Yes, your love was huge, but probably more than you ever realized, it was your unique and intimate admiration that won his heart. The way you looked up at him with your eyes full of admiration and affection, melted his heart. It has been said that every man does what he does for the admiration of one woman. You were that woman, and he bowed the knee and proposed. He felt deep feelings of love for you. Of course, when he failed to love you that first year of marriage as you expected, you stopped looking at him with a glowing face. You pulled back your expressions of respect. You didn't feel it. Your face turned sour. You blamed him for the negativity. Predictably, he withdrew more, and was less expressive of love, especially if he heard you say, "I don't respect you." This is why the Word of God commands wives to show unconditional respect. Her respectful behavior empowers her to energize her husband. Bottom line, it can prevent the marriage from going under. A wife has power. Peter was clear about that. The New International Version (N.I.V.) translates it, "... husbands ...may be won over without words by the behavior of their wives, when they see the... reverence of your lives." (1 Peter 3:1,2).

Do you wish your husband would respond again like he did early on? In courtship, we've concluded that your husband felt you loved him because you admired who he was as a human being. He felt you loved him because you believed in who he was as a man. He felt you loved him because you expressed awe over who he was deep within himself. You glowed with reverence at times. He felt you loved him because you honored him on a regular basis. This ignited feelings of affection and love in his heart toward you. This can happen again if you want it to! If he is good willed toward you, watch what takes place.

"for we have regard for what is honorable, not only in the sight of the Lord, but also in the sight of men."
- 2 Corinthians 8:21

Are you game? Let's take a test. It's very simple. You'll see your husband respond at some level with an act of service. If you look for it, you'll see it. It may be big or it may be small, but if he's good-willed, it will be there. Remember, when respected for who they are, men serve and die.

THE Test

The Test You'll Want To Take!

Didn't you hate those brainiac kids in school who did so well on tests that they seemed to almost look forward to taking them, just so they could show off to the rest of the class about how smart they were? Most of us hate tests. But here is a test you should absolutely want to take, because it's almost impossible to flunk.

We call it "The Respect Test" and it was designed especially for those of you who earnestly desire to act on this information but are experiencing cold feet. Taking the Respect Test will encourage you by giving you a taste of how your husband will respond. For wives who have been conditioned by modern culture to avoid this sort of thing, this is a great way to stick your toe in the water before jumping in (though God's Word is not an option to obey, is it?).

So what is the Respect Test? It's simply this. When your husband seems relaxed and has nothing particular going on, say the following to him: "I was thinking of you today. I was thinking of the things I respect about you. I want you to know that I respect you." That's it. Then exit the room. Don't stare at him; don't wait for his response. Say it and then quietly leave the room. Then watch what happens.

One wife told us that she followed her husband into the bedroom after he got home one day and said, "I was thinking of you today. I was thinking of the things I respect about you. I want you to know that I respect you." Then she turned to leave. When she got to the door, he screamed, "Wait! Come back! What things?" He was so loud that their children came running, as though there must be a pony in the bedroom! After the kids left, she too started to walk out. But with a loud whisper, he said, "Wait. Wait. Come back! What things?" He was riveted on her. She proceeded to tell him several things. After she was finished, he said, "Wow. Hey, can I take the family out to dinner?"

The wife told us that her husband *never* takes the family out to dinner. What was going on? What was this man doing? As we have said before, a man's first and fundamental impulse is to serve. Men serve in response to honor. The wife expressed her thanks but asked for a rain check since the kids had commitments that evening. She left the room but said 15 minutes later she heard pans banging in the kitchen. Her husband fixed dinner. She told me that he *never* fixed dinner. *Never.*

Again, he was serving.

A few days later we received another e-mail from her. She said, "You won't believe it. He's in the laundry room!" She then asked me, "Do you have any other 'respect tests?' Literally, I think I am going to get a cruise out of this."

Is this manipulation? Of course it can be, and a wife has to check her motivation before God in anything she does. But none of this is manipulation if a wife is sincerely expressing respect for who her husband is as a man. We will say it again and again: a good-willed husband serves when he feels his wife respecting him for who he is. That's the way he is made, and sometimes wives are shocked to see it actualized in their own marriage. Don't be shocked, be glad, and rejoice in knowing that you are reaping the benefits of obeying God's Word to you.

Another wife wrote us after a Love and Respect Marriage Conference: "Thank you for an absolutely uplifting experience. It was God-sent and exactly what my husband... and I needed. I praise Him for sending you out on this journey to strengthen marriages... Several times throughout the seminar my husband and I would reach out and squeeze each other's hands when something you said really affected us. A couple times I looked over at him to make sure he was listening and he had tears in his eyes!" Why the tears? He was hearing his mother tongue. And hearing one's mother tongue, after months and years of not hearing it, is profoundly affecting. It would be like being in a foreign country for years and suddenly bumping into someone who speaks English. You wouldn't let them go. You'd want to buy them dinner and spill your guts to them. That's the way it is with respect language. Upon hearing his mother tongue, a husband's spirit is deeply touched, and suddenly it can overflow with tenderness, affection and responsiveness to his wife.

You should believe this not because we say this, but because Scripture reveals it. Yes, we know, "This is so foreign." But will you question God's Word? We must always ask which we will trust, our feelings, or God's revealed Word? It is shocking news to most

> **"...everyone who hears these words of Mine, and acts upon them, may be compared to a wise man, who built his house upon the rock."** - Matthew 7:24

wives, but it is nonetheless entirely true. God's Word is clear. Perhaps for some, **this is really a crisis of faith**, not marriage.

During the breaks at our conferences, wives will often go to their husbands and say, "Is that how you feel?" They find it next to impossible to believe they could live with a husband these many years and not know he has such a deep-seated need to know and feel that she respects him. She finds it hard to accept that he wants to hear her say, "I was thinking about you today and all the things I respect about you." Depressingly, some hope their husbands will say it isn't how he feels. They feel that if he says he feels this way, it is an indictment on them as wives. Some wives feel they have this marriage-thing very well figured out, and he is the issue because he is less loving than she is. It is like living in a summer home only to discover at the end of August that a certain path led to a gate hidden by overgrown weeds and trees. Opening the gate and walking further, it led to a secluded, white sand beach. Oh, to have missed this!

Wives are usually convinced they understand everything about their husbands. So when they hear this information out of left field it can be very intimidating. When he says, "Yes, that's exactly how I feel," they are stunned and are tempted to say, "That's ridiculous. I am not going to respect you. You are not superior to me. I am not bowing to you." In order to avoid hearing this from their men, some wives won't even ask, "Is this how you feel?" If they do broach it, some might say, "I'm reading about this stupid idea that men need respect. In my opinion that is so arrogant. Don't you agree? Men don't deserve respect. This will set the feminist movement back fifty years." Such wives have become all too comfortable with expressing whatever they feel to their husbands. The sad truth is that some wives simply don't want it to be so, and they frame the issue in such a way that the husband has to agree with their sentiments. If the question is framed in that way, a husband will almost never open up and say, "Yes, that's how I feel." He knows his wife will show him contempt if he does!

But framing the question this way to your husband is comparable to a husband saying, "I'm reading about this stupid idea that fat women are hypersensitive to body image and being told they are fat. Are you really sensitive about being and looking so fat?" The difference is that a wife who is hurt and provoked in that manner will lash out verbally in response. "I can't believe how unloving you are!" But a husband who is hurt and provoked will probably go silent when told he is pathetic for needing respect. He feels he has no right to say, "You need to respect who I am as a man." If he did express that, he's afraid his wife would scoff at him. This is tragic. One day, though, if this wife has a son, and he marries a woman like his mother, she'll awaken to the scourge of contempt. She may observe her son's spirit die in his marriage. She will be one sad woman as she watches her son experience life like a child who suddenly becomes deaf, never again hearing what he used to hear with such pleasure. She may also then realize that her husband, too, is a son, and within him is a person longing to hear what God designed him to hear, but silence alone is his plight. As best he can, as he goes out into the world, he resists "the...woman...who flatters with her words" (Proverbs 2:16). But it would be far, far easier for him to resist that temptation if the woman he pledged his life to would lift him up with words of respect. Oh, how he longs to hear that someone admires him for who he is!

Let's go back to the Respect Test. When a wife walks into a room and tells her husband that she has been thinking about several things she respects about him, most husbands – after regaining consciousness and picking themselves up off the linoleum – will instantly ask, "What were you thinking? What do you mean? What do you respect about me?" A wife needs to be prepared to genuinely answer these questions. It isn't good enough to make a flat respect statement and then head for the hills and hope he doesn't mention it again. Trust us, that won't happen. But some women we've engaged on this subject say they don't know what to say to these questions. They actually say there isn't anything they really respect about their husbands. (This is comparable to him saying there isn't anything about her he loves). But no matter how bad a marriage is, and no matter how much a wife thinks there isn't anything she respects about her husband, there is plenty she respects, if she will only think about it honestly. First of all, every husband is created in the Image of God, so there needs to be a residual effect in him somewhere. Why does Jesus command us to love our enemies? Because they are made in God's image, and because He loves them. Can you see your husband in that light? God's Word commands us to see each other in that light, and Peter and Paul specifically command it with regard to husbands. Still, when some wives try to focus on this, they make a list of things they secretly want him to change. For instance, she has on her list to tell him she respects him as a good father. When asked, "Do you respect him for who he is as a father?" some say, "No, not really. He needs to change."

There's no reason to lie. That really is manipulative and it won't do. Instead, look at some of the areas that are obviously important to your husband. For example, he has a deep desire to work and achieve, a deep desire to provide for and protect you, a deep desire to be strong and to lead, a deep desire to analyze and solve, a deep a desire to do shoulder-to-shoulder activities with you, and a deep desire to be intimately and sexually connected to you. Even if in some of these areas he could improve – even if there is something in each of these areas that bothers you, that makes you feel unloved – try to see the part of him that needs to feel you respect him. Look at his desires, not his performance. You did in courtship. Try to see the image of God in him. The point of the Respect Test is to express your respect for his longings in these areas. Remember Jesus looked at the spirit of his disciples. Even though their flesh was weak, He saw their spirit as willing (Matthew 26:41). Look at your husband's spirit, not his weak flesh.

"Honey," you might say, "I respect the fact that you have a desire to get up every day and go to work. That is not an option for you. You have to do this, and you do it." Or, "Honey, I respect you for your desire to protect me and provide for me and the family. I think of all the insurance you have for us. I know that weighs on you at times, and I admire you for your commitment." Or, "Honey, I respect you for your desire to be the kind of leader God wants. I was

> "let the wife see to it that she respect her husband."
> - Ephesians 5:33

thinking of your interest in that retreat for men on the topic, 'How to be God's Man in an Ungodly World.'" Too many wives have confessed they focus on the negative, and don't want to see the positive. Yet, the positive is there. For example, we've had wives tell us their husbands are not spiritual leaders. Yet, the men are in church every Sunday, want to talk about prophecy, go on the men's retreat, volunteer to work at the church, and serve each year on a mission trip. What these women are saying is, "He isn't who I want him to be." But look at what God sees. Remember, the Lord may be more touched by your husband's heart than you think. If you have sons, how do you want your future daughter-in-law to feel toward him? Try to get in touch with your husband's good will, and express admiration for that. A good-willed husband is one who is not trying to displease his wife (1 Corinthians 7:33). He isn't intending ill will. He may not be as loving as he ought to be but he is *not* consciously, willfully and habitually trying to be displeasing. Remember, "Indeed, there is not a righteous man on earth who continually does good and who never sins" (Ecclesiastes 7:20). Though he gets mad and stubborn, he is not set on a course to hurt her. He sees himself as well meaning. He wants a happy marriage.

Even if the Respect Test doesn't work to your satisfaction, you should be convinced that the Word of God teaches unconditional respect. This means respect regardless of a husband's response.

What God says, not how your husband responds to the respect test, is the basis of showing unconditional respect. In learning to navigate by instrument panels, new pilots are put into spatial disorientation. When a friend of ours was trained, he was blindfolded in a pressurized cabin. At

> **"that your faith should not rest on the wisdom of men, but on the power of God."**
> -I Corinthians 2:5

night in a star-studded sky, he was turned upside down over a city. He didn't know he was upside down. When he looked "up," he was actually looking at the sparkling lights of the city but they looked like stars. When he looked "down" he was actually looking at the stars but it looked like the city lights. This is why the exercise was enacted. All of his feelings told him he was right side up, but when he looked at his instrument panel he blinked. It told him the plane was completely upside down. His brain and feelings were in absolute spatial disorientation. Pilots must make a life commitment to their instrument panel. They must reject their thoughts and go with the instrument panel. In the same way, God's Word about respecting your husband is God's instrument panel. Even if you feel differently or if after the respect test your husband doesn't respond as you feel he should, act in accordance with the Word of God. If the worldly wise tell you this is ridiculous, decide again if God is God in your life. Everyone will believe something on the basis of some "authority," whether that authority is a guru, personal experience, counselor, famous personality, professor, or family member, etc. Belief is inescapable. The question is, what will you believe and on what basis? You won't go wrong trusting Christ and the Scriptures.

When wives do the "Respect Test" things almost always happen. Men are starving for this. This is their mother tongue. One wife wrote, "Hi...I was at the MOPS meeting...this week when you spoke. I thought that you both were so interesting to listen to. I spoke with you just before you left about telling my husband on his cell phone that I respected him, then hanging up and waiting for his reply. Well, I did the test but not according to my original plan. Instead I typed up a little card (had to add hearts to it) on the computer telling him how much I respect him for working so hard to provide for our family and letting me be a stay-at-home mom for our three daughters. I then tucked it into his briefcase that was in his car ready for work the next day. He found it mid-morning. When he did, he called me and thanked me for making his WHOLE day. His last words before hanging up were...the predicted...I Love You. That was pretty fun to see that this worked just as you had said it would. Then the plot thickens. As predicted by you once again, that I would call a friend, I did. My friend and I (she was at MOPS too) laughed ourselves silly when I called her right away to tell her the results of our test. She told me she would gladly accept the flowers that I would surely be getting later in the day. No flowers came but it was still a fun experience. Thank you for helping me communicate my appreciation to my husband in a different and unexpected way. I know that he liked it!!!!" She signed the note to us, "Admiringly, (her name) :)."

His Need Versus Her Need

Ephesians 5:33 shows that just as a wife needs love, so a husband needs respect. As she needs love like she needs air to breathe, so he needs respect like he needs air to breathe. Peter was very clear about this in 1 Peter 3:2. But we don't merely find this in Scripture. Other authorities on marriage and male-female relationships have attested to it as well. In his book, **Solid Answers**, Dr. Jim Dobson writes, "In general, however, they want to know they are respected and honored by their wives, just as their wives want to know that they are loved...Again, the basic needs of each gender are straightforward. Women need to be loved, all year round, and men need to be respected, especially when the going gets tough. That understanding is hardly new. In fact, it is ancient. Here's the way the apostle Paul described it nearly two thousand years ago: 'Each one of you (men) must love his wife as he loves himself, and the wife must respect her husband' (Ephesians 5:33). Love and respect. It's an unbeatable combination" (pgs. 392, 395).

Dr. John Gottman, one of the world's foremost authorities on marriage, who studied two-thousand couples over a period of twenty years, and who can personally predict with 91% accuracy if a couple will divorce after listening to them for a few minutes, wrote the following in his book **Why Marriages Succeed or Fail**: "In our study of long-term marriages we recruited couples from a wide range of backgrounds who had been married twenty to forty years to the same partner. Despite the wide differences in occupations, lifestyles, and the details of their day-to-day lives, I sense a remarkable similarity in the tone of their conversations. No matter what style of marriage they have adopted, their discussions, for the most part, are carried along by a strong undercurrent of two basic ingredients: love and respect. These are the direct opposite of - and antidote for - contempt, perhaps the most corrosive force in marriage" (p. 61). Love and respect are the key ingredients! Add to that Gottman's assertion, that contempt may be the most damaging thing to marriage.

> **"Be devoted to one another in brotherly love; give preference to one another in honor..."** -Romans 12:10

As one reads Gottman, one recognizes that it is the wives who usually tend to complain and criticize and the husbands are the ones who usually get defensive and stonewall. Though not always the case, this is generally true. We have observed it in our own experience with couples. Our interpretation for why this is so is that the wife generally feels unloved – and the husband feels disrespected. When a wife feels unloved, she moves toward her husband aggressively to resolve the conflict. She will confront in order to *connect*. She will vent negatively, complaining and criticizing in order to resolve issues and reconcile. When asked why, she will indicate she is seeking to do the

> "It is better to live in a desert land, than with a contentious and vexing woman." -Proverbs 21:19

loving thing. The husband, on the other hand, tends to get angry and pull back. To him it feels like she confronts in order to *control*. He goes quiet and withdraws. When asked why, he may not immediately know but will indicate that he is trying to calm down. As he reflects he says that he feels she is scolding him. He feels her disapproval and contempt.

Biblically, Paul and Peter were gender specific. As a husband is commanded to love his wife, so a wife is commanded to be respectful.

> "...since she is a woman..." -I Peter 3:7

Apparently a husband is less natural at loving and more natural at respecting, and a wife is less natural at respecting and more natural at loving. Yes, a husband needs love and a wife needs respect. But God's Word does not command a wife to agape-love her husband. God designed her to agape-love. He doesn't need to tell her to do what He created her to do. That would be redundant. It is her nature to nurture! A wife will agape-love more naturally than her husband. Apparently, though, a wife does not react respectfully when there is conflict, especially when she feels devalued and unloved.

> "But we proved to be gentle among you, as a nursing mother tenderly cares for her own children."
> -I Thessalonians 2:7

She may not be mean but she can be mad. She may not be violent but she can be venomous. Respect is less natural for her. That depth of emotion she feels manifests itself as disrespect. God knows this and so He gives her a divine nudge in the right direction, a divine command to do what will bless her. As a woman of God, she is to take this by faith.

Some of you who really know the scriptures are wondering, what about Titus 2:4 and 1 Peter 3:7?

Titus 2:4   **that they may encourage the young women to love their husbands, to love their children,**

I Peter 3:7   **grant her honor as a fellow heir of the grace of life, so
that your prayers may not be hindered.**

What do they have to say about a husband needing love and a wife
needing respect or honor? Amazingly, the Greek words for love are entirely different than what you might expect. Titus 2:4, in which older women
are to encourage younger women to love their husbands and love their
children, uses the Greek word *phileo,* which indicates what is called phileo-
love or friendship love, not agape-love. As you may know, there are different kinds of love described in the New Testament.   In other words,
almost all wives and mothers give their families unconditional love, but
readily confess they can become very negative and unfriendly in the home.
Toward the husband, she will readily admit she loves him, but often does
not like or respect him.

I, Sarah, realized I was becoming a negative person in my home. One
day, Emerson said, "Sarah, I know you love me but I don't feel you like
me." I'm a very positive, upbeat person. If you ask any of my friends, I
know that's how they would describe me. I do see the brighter side of life.
But I was becoming negative in my home. I was seeing the glass half
empty instead of half full. I took my daughter on a trip to see my mother,
and the two boys stayed at home with Emerson. While I was gone, I felt
like God was really convicting me about this. I felt like there was just
something missing in my relationship with Emerson. The Lord spoke to
me about that, and I thought, "Lord, I need to make a choice. I'm going to
dwell on the positive, not the negative." I mean it was so bad that I was
complaining about the crumbs on the counter, the towels on the floor, the
shoes in the doorway, all of those kinds of things. I would make an issue of
everything.

I returned from my mom's house and said, "So, did you miss me?" He
didn't directly answer the question. He said, "You know, we just had a
great time and got along fine. Everything went well. We ate when we
wanted to eat. We made the beds when we wanted to make them. (I think
it was just before I came home.) Everybody got along. We built forts, and
those kind of things." I thought, "This is confirmation to me. He didn't
answer the question. He didn't miss me. It is time for me to change." I

needed to make that change. I wanted to be his friend. I married him because I liked him. We now know this is a major problem in many homes. Some wives are living in direct disobedience to Titus 2:4. Many "reasons" can be cited for the negativity. The fact remains God calls mothers of young children in particular to a friendlier approach in the home. In the home, and there alone, with her husband and children, she has become disapproving, downbeat and pessimistic. Only unconditional respect can counter this negativity.

We also need to note: in 1 Peter 3:7 where husbands are commanded to honor their wives as fellow heirs, it's a different term than the phrase "respectful behavior" used in 1 Peter 3:2. To honor her means to value her as an equal – a fellow heir. On the other hand, respect toward a man entails looking up to him as one who has the responsibility to be the protector, provider, overseer or head. That's the point of Ephesians 5:33. No wife wants to be looked up to as both the provider and protector of her husband. That's a turn off to her. Remember, Peter described the wife as "the weaker vessel" (1 Peter 3:7). She doesn't want to be the defender from outside forces. Does a wife realize how meaningful it is to a man to be viewed as the responsible, stronger vessel called to protect his wife? The notion of him being the Knight in Shining Armor isn't going away any time soon. The desire to rescue her as the Princess is deep within his soul, and that he wants to be admired as the rescuer is part of his psyche. And what little girl is indifferent to the princess motif? It's not politically correct, but it coincides with Scripture and experience; it is the stuff of the movie industry, despite the occasional Superwoman theme. When a wife lays down her cultural ideologies, and appreciates her husband for this in the home, most men are energized to love, serve and even die. When this respectful attitude comes from the wife, it motivates even disobedient husbands to come back to God (1 Peter 3:1,2). This is not reducing a wife's power but increasing it. She must, though, take that by faith.

Interestingly, to Peter, a husband is to be respected (1 Peter 3:1,2) despite his performance, even despite his disobedience to the Word of God. He may or may not be worthy, but he sees himself as a leader and responsible. On the other hand, a wife is to be honored because of who she is, a fellow heir of the grace of life and since she is a woman (1 Peter 3:7). She yearns to be considered his equal, harmoniously walking through life as one. We might simply say, she wants to be honored as equal and loved as first in importance to him. He wants to be respected as first among equals and liked as a good friend. If that happens, the marriage will be joyful! There is something very revealing about the different words that are used. God knows exactly with whom He is dealing. He created us male and female: He should know!

Understanding the True Nature of the Problem

The key to finding a solution is to understand the true nature of the problem. But what is the problem? We now know that the real problems are usually not what we think! Dr. Gottman asserted this himself. Though issues like sex, money, in-laws, children, work, chores, etc. are real, they are not the root. "If problem solving isn't the main goal of my recommendations, then what is?" Gottman asked. "The major goal is to break the cycle of negativity..."

In other words, based on Ephesians 5:33, we are setting forth the simple idea that a husband's negative, unloving reaction deflates his wife. If he overcomes that tendency, all will be well in her heart toward him, regardless of other problems. Do you, as a wife, see that? Even if, for instance, he is seeking to solve a conflict about money, it is his lack of

> **"...my heart is wounded within me."** -Psalm 109:22

> **"...her soul is troubled within her."** - 2 Kings 4:27

love that closes off his wife's spirit. When a husband yells, "Where's that $500!?" his wife is hurt. The money problems do not cause a breach of trust between them. It's his unloving demeanor that crushes her. Many husbands have money problems, but those men who come across lovingly, or who rebound by seeking forgiveness for being unloving, will be okay.

> **"When the heart is sad, the spirit is broken."** -Proverbs 15:13

And of course, on the other hand, a wife's negative, disrespectful reaction deflates her husband's spirit. If she overcomes that tendency, all will be well in his heart toward her, regardless of other problems. For example, even though she's trying to resolve a matter about a domestic chore, it's her lack of respect that closes off his spirit. She might say, "You never help. You're a lazy bum. You only care about yourself!" The fight over household chores isn't rupturing the relationship, as real as that is. It is her disrespectful demeanor that quenches him. If a wife confronts the issue respectfully, she will protect the marriage. "Honey, I am feeling overwhelmed. I need your help. I know you are exhausted, as am I, and some of this is unmanly, but would you help me tonight? I need your help in three areas." Sarah shares, "I would try to do it all and wait to ask for help until I was overly tired and frustrated. I would then come across disrespectfully. I also expected Emerson to discern what needed to be accomplished. As I saw this as a pattern, I engaged Emerson earlier on in a respectful manner. I also allowed for Emerson's standard of doing something to be one level below my own. He wouldn't get every crumb picked up like I would. Or, he would not see a dirty dish left on the table."

We have also introduced humor at this point. Emerson might claim the dish wasn't there but reappeared. Or, Sarah would say with a twinkle, "And what were you going to do with this dish?" And Emerson would say, "Oh, I was just going to wash that." We have tried very hard to keep humor front and center, not to make the other laugh as much as guide our own frustration. That negative energy needs to be channeled, and we have found there is a "time to laugh" (Ecclesiastes 3:4) and that time needs to come at some point during tension. As a wife, you can do this for yourself! You can bring healing. "A cheerful heart is good medicine" (Proverbs 17:22).

"She is boisterous and rebellious, Her feet do not remain at home;" - Proverbs 7:11

We have also introduced a phrase into our marriage: "You can be right, but wrong at the top of your voice." Our tones, facial expressions and attitude can close the other off far and above the content. Whether we like it or not, our countenance too often reveals our hearts –

"An excellent wife is the crown of her husband, But she who shames him is like rottenness in his bones." - Proverbs 12:4

at least it feels this way to a spouse. Characteristically, what we say is far less impacting than how we say it. The problem, of course, is if a wife feels she is seeking love by saying, for instance, "Talk to me!" she may not see her disrespectful sour look. If a husband feels he is doing the honorable thing by going quiet, he may not see how unloving that feels to her.

Having said this, since love and respect are the root issues, now let's ask a question. Is the problem the husband's lack of love or the wife's lack of respect? Well, of course the answer is both, as we have said and will continue to say. Both are responsible in God's eyes, period. But the reason we have written these things is because it is our sense, based on what we've seen in our marriage counseling, that the respect side has been ignored far more than the love side.

Are you teachable on this subject? Are you willing to allow God to gently lead you as you acknowledge this may be a serious problem? If you respond to God's solution, you do yourself a huge favor.

This is why we pray over 1 Thessalonians 2:13: "And for this reason we also constantly thank God that when you received from us the word of God's message, you accepted it not as the word of men, but for what it really is, the word of God, which also performs its work in you who believe." Our prayer is that wives will receive this teaching as God's revelation, not a human suggestion or option. When they do, it performs its work, as God's Word always does.

Some women are so convinced their husbands are the problem that they have become women of contempt. In the home some wives become spiteful and scolding. As one woman confessed in a conference, "Some of us have become venomous." In the home, and only in the home, some wives have become the boisterous, contentious, vexing woman of Proverbs toward their husbands (7:11; 9:13; 19:13; 21:9,19; 25:24; 27:15). Because they see them-

> "For it is not an enemy who reproaches me, then I could bear it; Nor is it one who hates me who has exalted himself against me, Then I could hide myself from him. But it is you, a man my equal, My companion and my familiar friend. We who had sweet fellowship together, walked in the house of God in the throng" -Psalm 55:12-14

selves as loving, and their husbands as less loving, they have rationalized their contempt. "There is no way I am going to be his dutiful, obedient, doormat wife!" they exclaim. Of course, that isn't the issue. God calls no one to be a doormat. The idea is related more to a simple attitude of honor. Peter wrote earlier in 1 Peter 2:17, "Honor all men." The call is for a wife to carry herself in dignity, showing honor to her husband because she is an honorable woman. Though her husband may not be respectable, God is calling her to show unconditional respect in her pursuit to obey God. She does this in obedience to the command of God in Ephesians 5:33, not because her husband deserves it. To do otherwise is an excuse. What do you think of the man who says, "I will not love my wife until she is lovable?" Thinking biblically, a wife does not cause her husband to be unloving but reveals him as an unloving person. He is disobeying Ephesians 5:33. So too, the Lord views a wife in the same way. It is not biblical to exclaim, "I will not respect my husband until he is worthy of respect." The truth is, a husband does not cause a wife to be disrespectful, but reveals her disrespectful demeanor. She is disobeying Ephesians 5:33. We have a phrase in our marriage: "My response is my responsibility." In other words, Sarah says, "Emerson does not cause me to be the way I am. He reveals the way I am. Therefore, if I am disrespectful, that's my issue and can't be blamed on Emerson. This is between God and me. God commands me to respect. In that sense, Emerson is irrelevant. So if I explode with contempt when he leaves his wet towel on the floor for the 565th time – this being the straw that broke the camel's back – my response is still my responsibility. I cannot justify my contempt because he has failed me."

Do you see the true nature of the problem? Are you ready to declare your allegiance to God's revelation? His truth has been etched on holy parchments. That truth won't change. Public opinion is not the voice of God. Though no one in our culture specifically addresses unconditional respect toward husbands, God does in the Holy Scripture. This is the voice of truth. This is the voice of God.

The Oxymoron About Respect

Many times wives have said to us, "I'm sorry, but I have never heard those two words put together, 'unconditional respect.' Isn't respect something one has to earn? It makes no sense that it should be unconditional." Many Christian wives, when hearing the phrase wonder if the concept of "unconditional respect" is biblical. That's an excellent question.

The Apostle Peter showed in 1 Peter 3:1, 2 that this husband is "disobedient to the word." In other words, he is either a carnal Christian or an unbeliever. In either case, he does not deserve his wife's respect. He has not earned it. He is not worthy of respect. We cannot stress enough that your husband may have serious problems. We are assuming he has good will but even if he doesn't, Peter clearly taught that by taking this approach of unconditional respect, you can turn him around. To be sure, Jesus had his Judas, so there are no absolute guarantees, but Peter was so bold about this that frankly this should be working more than it is. Probably it is not working because many wives are not obeying this revelation from God. For instance, if a husband truly loved his wife, few wives would resist, right? Yes, if she had transferred her affection to another man or was deeply bitter toward him it might not win her heart. Most women would testify, however, that such unconditional love over time would be hard to withstand. In the same way, few wives discern the power of unconditional respect toward a husband. The fact is, over time, few husbands can resist this. As love is her mother tongue, respect is his mother tongue. As love is music to her ears, respect is music to his ears. Sadly, feminism has taken the agenda to such an extreme that such a notion is repulsive. It is all about women and love, not about men and respect. But for that woman of faith and wisdom, such a divine revelation is a gift from God!

Not too long ago, Sarah encouraged a woman to see Emerson for counsel. She had recently placed her faith in Christ. She was having a serious problem in her marriage. Her husband was seeing another woman, and she didn't know what to do. Emerson listened to her circumstances and then asked her if she was interested in remaining in that marriage despite this grievous sin on her husband's part. She said that she was, emphatically so. "If that is the case," Emerson said, "drastic times demand drastic measures." He asked her if she was willing to try some things that many of her friends would say are foolish.

He then said, "For instance, there are a lot of divorced people out there, and they're not going to encourage you to remain in a relationship like this. It's very difficult for a divorced person to tell you to hang in there, and even if they wanted to, they'd feel it very inappropriate to ask you to do so. It would be like a bald man selling hair-growth tonic. There's a credibility crisis in situations like that. Even your friends who are still married may not encourage you to stay together, because our modern cultural mindset is that God wants you to be happy, and your friends want you to be happy, so far be it from them to suggest you stay in a relationship in which you must suffer. So they'll stay silent. But if you are willing to commit to some things here, even though everybody in the world will probably tell you you're stupid for doing so, you might be surprised at the results."

She said she was willing. She strongly wanted to keep the relationship, out of her love for her husband, and her commitment to her family. Emerson told her, "Well then, let's begin."

He communicated to her some of the information you are reading. He asked her to think about sending her husband a message of respect in a card. He asked if there was anything he enjoyed doing. "Yes," she said, "he likes boating." Emerson told her, "Well, let's think about that for a moment. I want you to communicate in an emotional word-picture of sorts, and say to him something in a manner that sends him the message of honor and respect." She thought for a moment, and then came up with a card that said something like this: "I want to thank you for being the ship and rudder in the storms of our life together." Then she signed it, "Respectfully, the one who still admires you."

We heard later that within minutes of receiving that card, he came to her with tears in his eyes. He held up the card and asked her, "Do you mean this?" She said, "Yes, I do." Continuing the motif, he told her, "I thought I was the hole in the boat." Then he asked, "Why are you saying this to me now?"

He knew some things were going on in her spiritually. She was attending a Bible study. Even so, he left for the state where the other woman lived. But six weeks later, he came running back. He burst into the house, screaming, "You have God! You have God! I want God!" He left the other woman, and today this couple is back together. Things don't always work out this way, but there is something deeply powerful that happens when a woman tells her husband that she respects him. We've seen it happen time and time again. Carl Rogers, the father of Rogerian counseling, used the phrase, "unconditional positive regard." He found that such an attitude is effective. He should. God's Word declared it 2000 years ago.

THE CONNECTION Between His Need & Her Need

The Crazy Cycle

When people act on God's promises, things happen. Unconditional love even won Hosea's wife Gomer (Hosea 3:1), who was an adulteress: "Then the Lord said to me, "Go again, love a woman who is loved by her husband, yet an adulteress, even as the Lord loves the sons of Israel, though they turn to other gods and love raisin cakes."

So too, unconditional respect can win disobedient husbands. Can Peter be any clearer?

In the same way, you wives, be submissive to your own husbands so that even if any of them are disobedient to the word, they may be won without a word by the behavior of their wives, as they observe your chaste and respectful behavior. - I Peter 3:1,2

Also, in Ephesians 5:33 the text does not read, "Husbands love your wives unconditionally and wives respect your husbands only if they have earned it." In other words, as a husband is to be a loving human being even if his wife is unlovable, so a wife is to be a respectful woman even if her husband is not respectable. We will say this again and again. A wife needs love. This isn't a personal wish; it's a deep need that resides at the core of her being. So too, a husband needs respect. This isn't an arrogant whim on his part, or some kind of chauvinistic attempt to declare superiority. It's a deep need, a cry from the bottom of who God created him to be. Often, it explains his anger.

> "...Rachel...said to Jacob, 'Give me children, or else I die.' Then Jacob's anger burned against Rachel, and he said, "Am I in the place of God, who has withheld from you the fruit of the womb?" -Genesis 30:1,2

Now for the love and respect connection.

If a wife feels unloved, she can react in ways that feel disrespectful to her husband. Then, when a wife is disrespectful, her husband tends to pull back, which feels even more unloving to her.

When a wife pushes her husband off her air hose connected to her love tank, she tends to step on his air hose connected to his respect tank. In other words, a wife's defensive reaction offends her husband who in turn gets defensive and offends her!

The beautiful reason God commands the wife to show unconditional respect is that this protects her against her tendency to be disrespectful when feeling unloved. A wife's natural thinking is captured in the declaration, "If he doesn't love me, there is no way I am going to show him respect. Absolutely not. He has to earn my respect. I'm not going to respect him until he loves me." But showing disrespect won't motivate him to feel fond feelings of love, any more than him being unloving motivates her to show respect. The revelation of God guards a wife against undermining the feelings of love in the marriage. Think about it. If disrespect de-motivates a husband from feeling fond feelings of love, then God knew exactly what He was doing! Peter taught that a husband can be won by a wife's unconditional respect. Her respect motivates his love! The Bible teaches that unconditional respect is highly motivational to a husband. Said another way, contempt toward a husband can result in him closing his spirit to his wife. No wife wants this.

What we discovered is a profound love-and-respect interaction. This is the secret that cracks the communication code in marriage! We call it the "The Crazy Cycle." (If you are interested in more information go to www.loveandrespect.com E-store.) The Crazy Cycle refers to the destructive cycle that is set into motion when a wife feels unloved or a husband feels disrespected. When the wife feels unloved, she usually reacts in a way that comes across as disrespectful to her husband. Then, when the husband feels disrespected, he usually reacts in ways that feel unloving to a wife. And so it goes, around and around and around. The Crazy Cycle is read: Without love she reacts without respect. Without respect he reacts without love.

To counter this downward spiral, a couple needs to get on what we've come to call "The Energizing Cycle." The Energizing Cycle refers to what happens when a husband is loving or a wife is respectful. When a husband is loving, it motivates his wife to be respectful or honoring. And when a wife is re-

spectful it motivates her husband to be loving and kind. The Energizing Cycle: his love motivates her respect; her respect motivates his love.

Predictably, many wives have told us that they love the idea of the Energizing Cycle. The Bible declares what happens in the heart of a wife when he loves her this way. "Prize her, and she will exalt you; She will honor you if you embrace her" (Proverbs 4:8). Naturally, a wife longs for her husband to treasure and embrace her. When he does this, she desires to admire and esteem him. But what should a wife do if her husband is not initiating with love – at least, not as she wants?

> **"The wise woman builds her house, But the foolish tears it down with her own hands."** -Proverbs 14:1

All too often, wives will say: "If he loves me, I'll respect him. Until then, no way." This, of course, doesn't accomplish much. The simple fact is– are you ready for this?– the one who sees himself or herself as the more mature will make the first move. If your husband is not initiating as you hope, you are not powerless in the situation. The Apostle Peter sees your unconditional respect as giving you a kind of spiritual authority, because you are doing as God commands. If you are the mature one, able to find your motivation in God's command to you, you can motivate and energize your husband. You can start a new cycle. Your respect will motivate his love. You have power to build into your marriage. It takes one to tango, and one to un-tango! There's no reason for you to wait for his love to motivate your respect. The biblical view is that you can act first. In fact, the biblical view is that you should act first, out of obedience to God, because your relationship with God precedes your relationship with your husband. To begin with, it's your relationship with God that gives you the ability to have a relationship with your husband.

Conversely, your disrespect neither wins him nor motivates his love.

And your love does not win him! Though that sounds like heresy, it is the biblical truth. Peter was clear on these two points. Because he said your "respectful behavior" wins a husband, then your disrespect and more love from you are emphatically *not* God's means for motivating your husband to change. It would be wonderful if your love for him changed him to the extent that unconditional respect does. Love is easier for you. But that isn't what God's Word says will happen. Respect is what he craves, and what motivates him, especially during moments of conflict.

Remember that during conflict he isn't shutting down and withdrawing because he feels unloved. He knows you love him. This is why after a conflict – unlike you – he does not seek reassurance of your love. He never doubted your love. (This is generally true for most men). He is stonewalling because he feels a measure of your disdain for him. He does not function well in the face of scorn. Actually, he needs reassurance of your respect but dares not ask for fear you will readily say, "I don't respect you during episodes like this. You need to change!" This equals a comment from him, "I don't love you during episodes like this. You need to perform!" At that instant, you feel an arrow go through your heart; so does he.

But we happen to believe once a wife grasps this, and begins to overcome her initial feelings of disbelief and fear, and at the same time allows her husband to have these feelings, they can begin a new dialogue that's enriching for them both. She will enter into his world of feelings, which she wanted to do but which she expected would be like her feelings. (By the way, he will have times when he wants to hear her expressions of love, and respond at that feeling level. We're not saying that doesn't exist, but we are saying this will increase if the contempt stops.) He will enter a new level in the marriage, which in some ways is a return to the days of courtship for him. As a wife reassures him that she is not seeking to scold and shame him but is crying out for his love, a husband can awaken to the spirit of his wife in a way that he has not done for years. If though, a wife keeps making comments about not respecting him for who he is, she'll push her husband away. After all, what wife keeps her heart open to a man who keeps repeating, "I don't know if I ever loved you?"

We know this entire message of respect is difficult to hear. Let's face it, in the last forty years we have become a love-dominated culture. Respect almost seems like an old-fashioned concept. We are awash in love-talk. Of course there's nothing wrong with love, but unfortunately it has often come at the expense of respect. Because of that, most wives have sought to love their husbands more, expecting their husbands to respond lovingly. But it hasn't worked that way and everyone has only gotten more frustrated.

Many wives think: "If he loved me like I love him, I'd change and be more loving and responsive." We agree, but that is a female speaking. Love is your mother tongue. Love is what energizes you. This feminine view has taken over the marital agenda. Husbands are incessantly told to love their wives. Husbands are to make their wives happy. A huge billboard in our city says, "Happy Wife, Happy Life." It's an advertisement for jewelry. There is truth here, as long as it's not one-sided. Remember, Eve had Paradise yet still wanted more. She was not happy! God Himself did not make Eve happy. Eve was deceived.

> "...respect, not only to those who are good and gentle, but also to those who are unreasonable."
> -I Peter 2:18

2 Corinthians 11:3 **But I am afraid, lest as the serpent deceived Eve by his craftiness, your minds should be led astray from the simplicity and purity of devotion to Christ.**

I Timothy 2:14 **And it was not Adam who was deceived, but the woman being quite deceived, fell into transgression.**

Even today, something exists in women that wants more from her world than her world can give her. In part this is there by God. She mothers her family to make them better. She wants the perfect Thanksgiving family time, the perfect Christmas time, the perfect family, and the perfect marriage. She is not satisfied. Some call this the insatiability of women. But if that standard is not met, she can become very unhappy. She can feel mistreated and even betrayed. When we add the last twenty-five years of teaching about a Happy Wife, a Happy Life, she can become resentful that her husband is not loving her enough, not changing enough. She can step over the line. Even Bible teachers select Scriptures to exhort husbands: "When a man takes a new wife...he shall be free at home one year and shall give happiness to his wife..." (Deuteronomy 24:5) But who is pointing out

to wives what Paul and Peter reveal? A husband is motivated most by his wife's respect because that is his need, but the focus is on love. The primary thing that motivates him is removed. The result is that he is not moving toward his wife to love her as she hopes. When she feels unloved, she reacts disrespectfully. When a husband is disrespected, he reacts even more unlovingly. Round and round it goes. Where it stops nobody knows!

As you read, we are answering the question: **How Does a Wife Motivate Her Husband to Love?** God's answer is unconditional respect. The challenge for every wife, of course, is to make a decision to move forward in obedience to God's command – to act on the words of Scripture. Regrettably, a wife can wait for her husband to show love before she shows respect. Certainly that's understandable. We teach that a husband's love motivates a wife's respect. There is a place for expecting a husband to be loving. But who hasn't taught this, talked about this, written a book about this, or done a seminar on this? Our culture is full of this message that husbands need to – and should – love their wives. Ultimately a husband must do this in obedience to God. If he doesn't, at least not to the extent that she expects, nonetheless the wife must clothe herself in respect. She must focus on God's command to her, not God's command to her husband. When she does, she stops a great deal of the craziness in the marriage. It is a law of Scripture, set forth by Peter in 1 Peter 3:1,2, that when a wife puts on respect, her husband changes. For some reason, this extraordinary revelation has been overlooked, and therefore, not taught as it should be, and many have suffered unnecessarily because of it.

> "Everyone who comes to Me and hears My words and acts on them, I will show you whom he is like: he is like a man building a house, who dug deep and laid a foundation on the rock; and when a flood occurred, the torrent burst against that house and could not shake it, because it had been well built." -Luke 6:47, 48

Ask yourself: When you feel unloved, do you react? Do you react disrespectfully? When your husband feels disrespected, does he react? Does he react unlovingly? **Do you see the love and respect connection?**

Without love you can react without respect. Without respect your husband can react without love. Sadly, those negative reactions can then be misunderstood by each of you. They are not decoded!

When you react negatively, your code to your husband is, "I feel unloved by you right now." Your code is obvious to you. However, if your reaction is disrespectful, your husband only hears, "I don't respect you." He then reacts unlovingly. Or, when your husband reacts negatively to you, his code is, "I feel disrespected by you right now." His code is obvious to him. However, if his reaction is unloving, you only hear, "I don't love you." You then react disrespectfully! **Round and round it goes.** The topics change but the crazy process repeats itself foolishly. Each spouse's negative reaction triggers even greater negative reactions.

When each negatively reacts, it is a cry that needs decoding. Painfully, your husband may not decode your code. As well, you may not decode your husband's code!

When you feel unloved as a wife, you negatively react. You know you are being negative, that's not the point. What you do not realize is that your husband interprets your negative reaction as *disrespectful*. This is the disconnect! To you, your negative reaction is purely defensive. To your husband, amazingly, you are coming across as offensive. You know you are crying out for love. You know you have good will. The code you are sending in your negative reaction, which is obvious to all women, is, "I feel unloved." Lamentably, your husband doesn't crack that code! He sees you as being on the attack.

And so when this happens – when a husband feels attacked and disrespected – he reacts negatively. He reacts in ways that feel very unloving to his wife. He does not want to. He has good will. In his heart, he trusts her but can't figure out why she has such a problem with him. And just as with his wife, a husband's *defensive* reaction ends up coming across as *offensive!* The code he is sending in his negative reaction is, "I feel disrespected." Unfortunately, a wife doesn't crack that code. Instead, she decodes his negative reaction to mean, "I don't love you." She is offended!

So, today's wife misses two things. She misses what her negative reactions mean to her husband. He hears, "I don't respect you." Also, she misses what his negative reactions mean to him! "I am trying to tell you to stop being so disrespectful." Instead of decoding this, she is insulted when her husband does not understand her negativity, claiming, "He doesn't get it!" And then she is really insulted when her husband wants her to stop being so disrespectful, claiming, "He's the problem, not me!"

When a wife accepts what God's Word is saying about respect and applies it, her husband starts hearing her need for love in new and exciting ways! Let's face it, isn't this exactly why God spoke this message through his servants, Paul and Peter (Ephesians 5:33b; 1 Peter 3:2)? Wasn't it to bless wives?

Ephesians 5:33   **Nevertheless let each individual among you also love his own wife even as himself; and let the wife see to it that she respect her husband.**

I Peter 3:1, 2   **In the same way, you wives, be submissive to your own husbands so that even if any of them are disobedient to the word, they may be won without a word by the behavior of their wives, as they observe your chaste and respectful behavior.**

The Bible commands a wife to show respect in attitude and action because it really works – because wives will be blessed! When a wife comes across as respectful, not only is she obeying God, she is reducing the reason for negativity in the marriage. By awakening to God's revelation, she does herself a huge favor. Over time, this proves to be the wise choice to make. You can either challenge your husband respecfully or disrespectfully. Which one makes more sense?

Let's put it this way. There are two coaches. One coach is Bobby Knight, former head basketball coach at Indiana University. The other is the head coach at the University of Kansas, Roy Williams. Both challenge their players. Bobby Knight is "in your face," belligerent, and boisterous. He was fired because the decision-makers finally got fed up with his disregard and disrespect toward others. He challenged players and administration disrespectfully. When people sense you have contempt, even if you are the best at what you do, you finally wear people out. They get their fill.

Roy Williams, on the other hand, is also a winner. He is rarely disrespectful, yet he challenges his players equal to Bobby Knight. So, when we promote the biblical teaching on respecting your husband, we are not saying cease your challenges. What we are advocating is to do it as Roy Williams does, not as Bobby Knight. Yes, Bobby Knight achieved his end, as can you, but what do you have?

You have every right to appeal to him to be more loving if you have been respectful. Men have an honor code. When you have been an honorable woman, it ignites in your husband a desire to be more loving. This is the law of honor to a man.

The question you need to ask is this: Am I going to wait until my husband puts on love before I act on this? We know some wives who have waited for decades. And we don't recommend it.

Remember our two stories earlier? The husband who bought his wife a birthday card, thinking it was an anniversary card? What about the couple distressed over excessive job responsibilities, upset over the broken garbage disposal, and anxious about getting a root canal at the dentist? As the conflict ensues in each story, the wife begins to feel unloved and reacts in a way that he feels is disrespectful. And when her husband feels disrespected, he reacts in ways that feel unloving. Neither decodes the code, and the Crazy Cycle continues to spin.

So, can we get off the Crazy Cycle? First of all, we should be clear that even though our goal is to avoid the Crazy Cycle altogether, we are all human, and even the very best couples will stumble onto it now and again. We are "in process" until we get to heaven. We say this because both of us still sometimes stumble onto the Crazy Cycle before we realize what's happening. No one can get off the Crazy Cycle absolutely. The goal is to reduce the number of times we spin on it.

> "**Not that I have already obtained it or have already become perfect, but I press on so that I may lay hold of that for which also I was laid hold of by Christ Jesus.**"
> - Philippians 3:12

In fact, just recently, returning from a conference in Greeley, Colorado, we were in a car trying to find the Denver airport. One sign said turn left, but when we took the left we discovered no more signs for the airport for miles and miles. Obviously we had made a wrong turn, so we went all the way back. When we got back to the road we had been on, we discovered we had been right all along and so we made the left again. But I, Emerson, was pretty frustrated as you might well imagine, and since I was the one behind the wheel, I floored the accelerator in anger and the car lurched forward, causing Sarah to spill hot tea on herself.

Needless to say Sarah was not pleased with me. If I had been a little more sensitive and hadn't gotten angry, I would not have reacted that way and floored the accelerator. Sarah wasn't in a great mood at this point, either, so she wasn't immediately forgiving. Let's just say that she kind of let me have it verbally. Maybe she kind of screamed at me. Or let's just speak directly: she didn't *kind* of scream at me, she absolutely and unequivocally screamed at me. With a lap of hot tea, she felt somewhat unloved – understandably so – and with an earful of hot words, I felt somewhat disrespected.

And it got even worse, because another sign told us to go straight, but in our confusion over the previous signs, and what with the hot tea and hot words flying around the car, we turned right instead! Needless to say I would have liked to have had a few hot words with the municipal road crews who had set up these signs. Maybe if I'd had the chance I might have thrown a cup of hot tea in their laps for good measure.

> "...fools display dishonor."
> - Proverbs 3:35

At one point Sarah was telling me to praise the Lord, but I really was in no mood to praise the Lord. But that's our sinful nature. We usually aren't in the mood to do what is right. We are usually in the mood to do what *feels* right. It felt right to floor the accelerator, to be unloving and inconsiderate to Sarah – and it felt right for her to scream, being disrespectful to me. Neither of us was right, and so, along with so many other couples that day, we went for a spin on the Crazy Cycle.

The point of the story is to tell you not to despair! If the Crazy Cycle happens to the folks who are writing about this subject – that's us – it just might happen to you now and again, despite your best efforts. Don't worry! Again, the short-term goal is to reduce the number of times we spin on it, and to reduce the length of our spins! We want to get to a point where we recognize that we're spinning and stop. That, in and of itself, would mean huge progress for anyone!

Our goal is not to stuff our feelings away, but neither is the goal to justify our own wrong reactions and blame each other for that negativity. At a certain point we both own up to our own foolishness. It is pointless in saying he or she is 51% responsible. Remember the basic rule: "My response is my responsibility. You don't cause me to be the way I am, you reveal the way that I am. Therefore, if my response is unloving or disrespectful, that is my sinful issue that needs to be confessed to Christ and you." We tend to lay blame for the first few seconds of a tiff, but relatively soon we own up to the matter. That is not easy, but it works.

We have found something else that works. If Emerson doesn't own up to his guilt, he usually comes under conviction. How so? If he doesn't apologize for being unloving, I, Sarah, apologize for my part on being disrespectful, even if he started it. I confess, "I was disrespectful. You don't deserve that, will you forgive me?" That may sound unfair to you but over time it usually convicts a person. Initially, your husband may retort sarcastically, "Well it's about time you admitted something." Let that roll off your back. If you confess your sauciness, he begins to awaken to his failure to be kind. He may respond less than you want. Emerson is not as expressive and responsive as I am. But over time he has responded far more than when we were first married. If you disrespectfully confront your husband for being unloving, demanding he confess, rarely does that work. Do you really expect him to acknowledge his lack of love when you disrespectfully blast him for being unloving? We have found when one of us confesses 30% of the guilt, the other comes around to confessing his/her 70%.

Is this counsel foreign? Well, ask yourself how ready you are to confess your disrespect. That's not a language you speak. You are willing to say you were unloving, but not disrespectful. One wife had us write that confession on a piece of paper. She kept forgetting the word "disrespectful." She asked, "What's the word again?" We were in disbelief! She couldn't remember the word "disrespectful!" So we said, "Can you say, 'I was unloving. I was wrong. You don't deserve that, will you forgive me?'" She said, "Oh, that's easy." We said, just replace the word "unloving" with the word "disrespectful." One would not think at first glance that this should be so alien. Our experience reveals otherwise. This whole concept, as central as it is to the heart of God, feels like gravel in a woman's mouth. It isn't natural. There was no rebellion in this wife. Love just so dominated her mind, body and soul that there was no room for this notion of respecting a man in a dignified way. Confessing disrespect was even further from her nature. Being

> **"Strength and dignity are her clothing..."**
> - Proverbs 31:25

> **"Render to all what is due them...honor to who honor."**
> - Romans 13:7

asked to speak these words was comparable to asking a Frenchman, who knew no English, to sing the Star Spangled Banner. But if a wife is ready to reduce the craziness, she can. God has revealed His truth to counter the Crazy Cycle. This truth empowers her. How badly do you want to decrease the marital craziness?

Etched in Parchment

Let's step back for a moment. Do you believe God has revealed this truth about love and respect? Do you see the implication of this in the Crazy Cycle, that there is a love and respect connection? Do you truly believe our loving Lord revealed to Paul His truth for the church on marriage? Do you believe this Revelation from God is the key to a successful marriage?

Prior to writing Ephesians 5:33: "Nevertheless let each individual among you also love his own wife even as himself; and let the wife see to it that she respect her husband," Paul had written, "that by revelation there was made known to me the mystery, as I wrote before in brief...which in other generations was not made known to the sons of men, as it has now been revealed to His holy apostles and prophets in the Spirit" (Ephesians

> **"Charm is deceitful and beauty is vain, But a woman who fears the Lord, she shall be praised."**
> - Proverbs 31:30

3:3,5). Was the truth in Ephesians 5:33 God's revelation? According to Paul, yes.

Did you know that Peter teaches that Paul spoke from God? As one reads the Scripture, a phrase is used hundreds of times. "The word of the Lord came to..." This word came to Moses, Samuel,

Jeremiah, Ezekiel, Isaiah, the minor prophets, and the list goes on. Peter describes what happened: "But know this first of all...men moved by the Holy Spirit spoke from God" (2 Peter 1:20,21). Peter continues by telling us that Paul's writings are "Scripture." Peter says, "just as also our beloved brother Paul, according to the wisdom given him, wrote to you, as also in all his letters, speaking in them of these things, in which are some things hard to understand, which the untaught and unstable distort, as they do also the rest of the Scriptures, to their own destruction" (2 Peter 3:15,16). The rest of the Scriptures – Peter views Paul's writings as Scripture, equal to the writings of Isaiah, Moses and David.

Because Peter's writing is also viewed as the Word of God, what do we make of both Paul and Peter revealing that unconditional respect is God's will for wives?

We know that a wife doesn't want to show unconditional respect, especially when her husband comes across unlovingly. Yet, Ephesians 5:33 and 1 Peter 3:1, 2 is God's revelation. If a husband does not respond, the command of God is not invalidated. The husband's response is irrelevant. The call of God is for the wife to trust and obey Him. God is calling her to love and

> **"All Scripture is inspired by God and profitable for teaching, for reproof, for correction, for training in righteousness..."**
> - 2 Timothy 3:16

revere Him. God will help every wife who seeks to trust and obey Him. As she places her confidence in the "inspired" Scripture, it will prove "profitable."

Peter said, "Husbands may be won without a word by the behavior of their wives, as they observe your... respectful behavior" (1 Peter 3:1,2).

> **"Honor all men..."**
> - I Peter 2:17

This is enormously motivational. When a wife acts on the Word of God something happens. When a wife shows respect in face and tone, it touches her husband's spirit. This is especially so when he knows he has been less than loving in response to a conflict. Respect empowers a wife to energize her husband. And this is toward a disobedient husband. Even more so with a good-willed husband!

When Peter reveals this, he is not calling you to respect your husband's person per se, but his position as husband. One female Christian counselor takes wives to Ephesians 5:33. She tells them, God "is asking us to respect our husband's position; the position God put him in as the head or covering of the family. As we explore what that means, most women can really relate to that and think of ways that she can respect the position her husband holds and separate that from the behavior that creates such frustration and anger." We've shared, "It is like the respect a four star general shows toward a five star general." That caused a light bulb to come on for one wife. It's like the respect a five star general shows toward an enlisted man. Colin Powell, Secretary of Defense, would never be disrespectful toward a corporal. Colin Powell shows respect whether others deserve it or not because Colin Powell has developed the ability to be dignified and respectful within himself.

The respect Peter addressed is like the respect we tell students today to show toward those who are culturally different from them. Though we differ, we do so respectfully. It is the respect all Christians are to show other people, whether it is toward the busy clerk behind the counter, the upset customer coming through the front door, or the IRS agent. Without question, some people are "more honorable" (1 Chronicles 4:9), and it makes this easier. If, however, we deem someone less than honorable, contempt isn't justified. We must treat everyone with respect, even those who don't deserve it – and yes, even husbands who don't deserve it.

Ephesians 5:33b and 1 Peter 3:2 is the clear Word of God. Even so, how easy it is to block it out when we don't want to hear something. Some turn to teachers who preach love and love as the only necessary requirement in marriage. These teachers and wives aren't interested in the fact that the "whole counsel of God" (Acts 20:27) on this subject is being ignored. When the Bible says the greatest of these is love, this is a comparison to faith and hope (1 Corinthians 13:13). Paul penned the Love Chapter, but does not command a wife to love – he commands her to respect!

Many godly and wise women – who themselves preach faith above feelings to others – for some reason have a hard time applying faith to

> **"For the time will come when they will not endure sound doctrine; but wanting to have their ears tickled, they will accumulate for themselves teachers in accordance to their own desires;"**
> - 2 Timothy 4:3

this issue between themselves and their husbands. For some reason, on this respect issue they go quiet. They have a hard time pursuing further insight on how to show unconditional respect to their husbands. This is not a topic of discussion over coffee. Anything else might be: love, relationships, family, feelings, clothing and weight-loss, but not the central summary of Paul and Peter on marriage, which is respect for husbands. When this happens, we have to ask ourselves, are we having a crisis of faith more than a crisis in marriage? Are evangelical women really women of the Word? Each needs to go before Christ on this. Too many women have little respect for their husbands and no one has pointed out to these women that this

> "..the woman being quite deceived fell into transgression."
> - I Timothy 2:14

reveals their disobedience to the Word of God. This isn't about their husbands; this is about them following Jesus. The encouraging thing is that when this is highlighted, many immediately introduce a change in their thinking and actions.

The question before us then becomes: Is this too simplistic? To reduce the problems in a marriage to the lack of love and respect is stretching it, isn't it? Aren't there many more problems than this? What would Paul say to a wife based on Ephesians 5:33b? What would Peter say based on 1 Peter 3:2? Both would say that in the midst of those problems you cannot forfeit the attitude of unconditional respect. If you do, this will create havoc in your marriage far more than the problems. Paul and Peter don't get into specifics but hit the essential attitude and action of unconditional respect. May we extend an invitation to you to make a decision to follow the Word of God? This isn't about your feelings but your faith.

Let's Call for the Vote

Board meetings! You've been in them. Much discussion takes place, and then the chairperson summarizes. The motion is read, and there is a call for the vote.

What's your vote? Are you ready to vote, "I will open my heart to God's truth on unconditional respect. I will do what I can, with His help, to slow down the Crazy Cycle. I will do what I can to motivate my hus-

> "To the pure, all things are pure; but to those who are...unbelieving, nothing is pure."
> - Titus 1:15

> "...who loathed their husbands..."
> - Ezekiel 16:45

> "Then she said to him, 'How can you say, 'I love you,' when your heart is not with me? You have deceived me these three times and have not told me where your great strength is.'" - Judges 16:15

> "...women...led on by various impulses..."
> - 2 Timothy 3:6

band God's way." Yea or nay?

Let's summarize and then call for the vote.

Today, the husband's need for respect has been removed from the marital radar screen. As one woman said, "We have been conditioned to believe men are basically pigs." It isn't that women want to believe this. Even so, when women feel unloved, they naturally feel disrespect. This seems to be a law of romance from a wife to her husband: "If I am loved by you, I will respect you. If I feel unloved by you, I can't feel respect and I won't show respect." A husband is not authorized to say, "If I feel disrespected by you, I can't feel love and I won't show love." Love is to be given unconditionally, whereas respect is to be earned.

Do we hear you agreeing? "That's true. That's what women feel."

What intensifies this negativity for the wife is her pink love lenses. A wife tends to see the presence and absence of love in the marriage.

She does not see her disrespect as that which is contributing to the lack of love in their marriage. Love is everything. If she feels unloved, he is unloving. If she is disrespectful, he is not respectable. Again, this is her law of romance. "Because I love you, you are to love me in return. My love for you is to trigger your love for me. If you do not love me, I will show you disrespect until you do love me. I don't want to be disrespectful, but you don't deserve respect. My disrespect is a wake up call for you to love me. It is rooted in my hurt. You should love me like I love you. If you don't there is something wrong with you. I know I am right because my feelings are so strong about this, and all my friends feel the same way."

Darin and Barb are both reading in bed. Barb is reading a magazine called "The Better Sex." She turns to Darin and says, "I'm reading an article you need to read. It explains why you're such a moron." Let's face it: male bashing is popular these days. We cannot really imagine a husband saying that he's reading an article that his wife needs to read, explaining why she's such a moron. Somehow jokes of that nature tend to be in one direction. Female-bashing jokes – except for the occasional blonde joke – don't fly nowadays. But male-bashing jokes are fundamental and accepted. A wife can say to her girlfriends, "I have four children. Three by birth, one by marriage." A husband cannot. Immersed deep within her soul is the belief that when she talks this way, her husband will awaken to her need to be understood and loved in better ways.

Are you a wife who is so fixated on love that you cannot see another way of viewing the marriage? To a hammer, everything is a nail. To a surgeon, every ailment is in need of surgery. To a nutritionist, food supplements are the answer. To a wife, marital problems are due to a husband's failure to love. To a wife, he caused her to feel unloved and he caused her to feel disrespect for him. If she feels unloved, he's to blame. If he feels disrespected, he's to blame! No wife wants to feel this way but when it is unpacked, this is what is happening. She is riveted on this as the explanation for their problems.

> "Because of your hardness of heart, Moses permitted you to divorce...but from the beginning it has not been this way."
> - Matthew 19:8

If you do not want to interpret things like this, are you ready to introduce positive changes? Are you ready to head in a new direction? You will need to vote to do so; that is, you will need to make a decision to head in that direction. Are you ready for the vote? Will you vote to halt the crazy cycle in your marriage?

Consider these issues before you vote: what if your husband is in serious disobedience? What if he is addicted to some sin? For instance, what if he is an adulterer? You may have grounds for divorce. However, did Peter have in mind these types of sins? Did Peter believe you could win your husband? If Peter were talking to you personally, would he invite you to put on unconditional respect toward your disobedient husband? Would he call you to enter into this spiritual discipline? Is God calling you? It won't be easy. But we have confidence in your faith and ability to follow God's leading.

Let's call for the vote. "I will open my heart to God's truth on unconditional respect. I will do what I can, with His help, to slow down the Crazy Cycle. I will do what I can to motivate my husband God's way." Yea or nay?

Is This Message an Answer to Your Prayers?

"An inconvenience is only an adventure wrongly considered; an adventure is an inconvenience rightly considered," wrote G. K. Chesterton (1874-1936). Is showing unconditional respect an inconvenience? On deeper reflection though, might it be God's invitation to enter an adventure? After all, would God command you to enter a journey that had no reward at the end or along the way?

When Peter was addressing marriage, he wrote about, "the holy women...who hoped in God..." (1 Peter 3:5). Is your hope in God? Could these pages in your hands be part of God's answer for you? Peter goes on to say, "For the eyes of the Lord are upon the righteous, And His ears attend to their prayer" (1 Peter 3:12). What about this verse? "I am a woman oppressed in spirit...but I have poured out my soul before the Lord" (1 Samuel 1:15). Does this describe you?

Has God been preparing you to hear this message? One wife wrote, "What a blessing the Love & Respect Conference was (& is) to us! We spoke to you on Friday night at the front desk and mentioned how excited we were. Well, it only got better after Saturday. I feel like I have received a precious gift – the ability to better understand my husband's deepest needs. I always wanted to meet them, but did not understand how respect felt to him the way love feels to me. We are committed to taking the principles and concrete ideas we learned and applying them to our marriage – and teaching them to our children so they can have better marriages right from the start. I have to tell you that the couples we spoke with (about six or so) all were excited by what you were sharing with us. We kept hearing story after story (and had a few ourselves) of the things that had happened in our relationships in the past six months that seemed to prepare our hearts for what you were telling us. God is awesome!"

There seem to be two basic responses from wives to this message. On one hand, there is a group that thanks God. One wife wrote, "I don't think that my husband needs to be more loving. I mean, yes, of course, sometimes I feel he is insensitive, but I honestly think that most of the time, it is I who need to be more respectful." (If you are in her camp, you will be helped immeasurably by what we write.) Even if she is not accurate, God will honor that. This reflects humility, and God exalts the humble. Even if your husband is more unloving than you are disrespectful, your new respectful attitudes will motivate him to be more loving. You won't lose when you act on this.

On the other hand, there is a group of wives who feel genuine hostility toward this message. We hear it sometimes: "I hated what they said," One wife commented. "I hated what Sarah shared and what Emerson said. There is no way I will ever show respect to my husband." Who wouldn't give mercy to a wife who had an evil-willed husband? We will allow for these sentiments to be expressed. But, most wives who express these things are married to good-willed men. Even this lady, we found out from other women, is married to a man who has never, ever abused her, and gives her everything. In fact, he is a man worthy of respect. Yet, he isn't the romantic she wants him to be, and she is bitter and gave this testimony. God have mercy on her from the other side. The contradiction between her attitude and her husband's behavior was staggering. So much for what our loving and glorious Lord Jesus revealed through Paul and Peter. In her view, if someone is not who she wants, she can express disdain, contempt, and scorn. To the true followers of Christ, that is incompatible with God's call on both men and women. Even so, this woman's vote was, "Nay."

INSIGHTS Into a Wife

Who Started It? A 19-Year-Old Male or a 19-Year-Old Female?

Who is more ready for marriage, a nineteen-year-old man or a nine-teen-year-old woman? In dealing with family related issues, she is, by three to five years. So, this guy's failure to love is rooted in his immaturity, not spite. He gets invited to play nine holes of golf with his buddies after work and doesn't tell her. She's still at work; it's no big deal, or so he thinks. He'll be late but not that much, so it will be okay. His mother always understood. He's not doing this because he's unloving. He lacks social graces. He will soon learn! He forgets her birthday and even the anniversary, not because he does not love her but because he doesn't think about birthdays and anniversaries like she does. Little girls dream about having a baby as well as a wedding day. This is part of her female psyche. Thus, birthdays and anniversaries are a natural fixation to her. He did not dream about tuxedos, and his mother always bought a birthday gift for him to give to his friend.

But back to our nineteen-year-olds. She fixes a meal for him and his three buddies, and then is in the kitchen afterward cleaning up while he's playing video games with his friends. After they leave, a huge fight en-sues. She throws a boot at him while he sits there alone playing another game. She lets him know in no uncertain terms that he's selfish, insensi-tive and unappreciative: "You don't love me!" He feels ashamed. He feels humiliated by her words. But were his actions due to immaturity?

When women say, "Men don't get it," there is some truth here. Yet if she shows contempt, he'll shut down. From his vantage point, she started it. From her angle, he did. A mature nineteen-year-old woman can view his actions as very hurtful, and then spitefully show disrespect. She doesn't see the damage her disrespect does because she thinks he deserves this, that it will motivate and change him. Yet when contempt is shown toward an immature nineteen-year-old male, he'll get angry and shut down. This couple is now on a cycle of criticism and withdrawal. Both feel justified in reacting the way they do. She feels she's trying to do the loving thing by confronting the issues so they can reconcile. She may be disrespectful, but he is far more unloving. He feels he's trying to do the respectful thing by not letting himself be provoked and fighting with her. He may have been unloving, but he didn't intend to be, whereas her disrespect is intentional and mean.

So, who started it? Yes!

Let it be added, that if a city was attacked, do you want five thousand nineteen-year-old women defending the city, or five thousand nineteen-year-old men? A nineteen-year-old male is the perfect fighting specimen. His eye-hand coordination, ability to fight, and his commitment to do the honorable thing make him the better choice by far. And just as she would struggle being a warrior fighting hand to hand combat to defend the city, which a male has less trouble with, he has a struggle to love as she loves. He is less natural at it.

So, who started it? Again, it all depends on one's frame of reference and criteria. Pink is correct if the focus is on love. Blue is correct if the focus is on respect.

The Chicken or the Egg?

Blame placing was the first sin after the first sin. We read in Genesis 3:12, 13, "And the man said, 'The woman whom Thou gavest to be with me, she gave me from the tree, and I ate.' Then the Lord God said to the woman, 'What is this you have done?' And the woman said, 'The serpent deceived me, and I ate.'"

Adam wasn't to blame; God and Eve were. In one sentence he blamed the only two beings he knew! Eve blames the serpent. So, who did God hold more responsible? Yes! Both were cursed. Both entered sin. Both were on their way to Hell apart from a Savior.

At this point, we are confronted with the proverbial chicken-or-egg question. In your case, who started it, your husband or you? Who does

God hold more responsible? Naturally you feel that your husband started it by being unloving. And naturally he thinks – when he thinks about it – you started it by being disrespectful. Or even if he admits that he started it by his thoughtlessness, he now feels that you feed the marital problems with your negative, disrespectful attitude. Who decides where the blame is to be placed? Scripturally speaking, everyone is guilty. None of us has an out. You both started it and God holds you both responsible. God expects you to behave lovingly and respectfully no matter how you are treated, period. Remember, God designed women to love more naturally. That's easier for you. It is less natural for you to show respect or see your disrespect. God designed your husband to respect more naturally. That's easier for him. It is less natural for him to show love or see his failure to love. Thus, each is responsible to obey God's Word at the point of unnaturalness. How easy it is for you to rationalize your disrespect when feeling unloved. Further, how easy it is to see yourself as better because you love more naturally – to God's credit, we might add! But what does the Lord feel about your disrespect?

So, who started it? To understand the situation a bit more fully, let's take a look at the larger cultural picture for a moment. For the last forty years – essentially since the Sixties – Western culture has viewed romance and marriage issues, and much else, through the pink-tinted lenses of love. Who could argue with that? Love posters, love children, the Summer of Love, and love-ins hit the American continent like a tidal wave. We said "Make Love, Not War" – as if that was the only choice available, and before long the idea of love became a kind of panacea. Love really had become the answer in many people's minds. That melody resonated with the spirit of women. It isn't that love is unimportant to men. It is huge. But, as we've been preaching, when your husband negatively reacts to you, rarely if ever is he feeling unloved. That's not the issue when the issue isn't the issue!

Even so, because "love" is what matters to most women, when someone comes across as unloving, we are very quick to spot it as the problem. And it is a problem when someone is unloving, a big problem, but it's not the *whole* problem, it's just the part that we tend to focus on. As a result, when marital conflicts arise, it's a wife's natural tendency to make the case against her husband. You exclaim, "The problem is his failure to love, not my failure to respect. Love is more important than respect!" Paul, who penned the Love Chapter, would not agree. Peter, who walked with the Lord of Love for three years, would not agree either. He commands her to show respectful behavior. This is the secret revealed!

> **"The wisdom of the prudent is to understand his way."**
> - Proverbs 14:8

What we're trying to communicate to wives is that although she probably is better at loving, her disrespectful reactions – which she isn't paying very close attention to – are canceling the love out! The disrespect outweighs the love and she's no better off than where she started. Said another way, her deposits of love are weighty, but her disrespect can emotionally bankrupt the marriage. Or to put it yet another way: An ounce of disrespect can outweigh a pound of love!

Listen to Solomon, the wisest man who ever lived: "Dead flies make a perfumer's oil stink, so a little foolishness is weightier than wisdom and honor" (Ecclesiastes 10:1). Your foolish disrespect can be weightier than your wise love. This is the problem!

We can argue until we are blue in the face that he started the conflict with his unloving demeanor – that he is far more responsible. That's been the argument for decades in this culture. And each marriage must be evaluated individually. Some men are unloving and the wives are respectful, and he is totally responsible. We have seen this. But is this the sole explanation to a 50% divorce rate in the United States? The other side of this says that if a wife comes across as having contempt, a husband will continue pulling back. That's the ugly fact of the matter. If that downward, negative spiral isn't halted, the marriage will crash and burn.

A Woman's Glow During Courtship

Why did your husband propose to you? When you fell in love with him, he walked into the room and there was a glow in you toward him. Do you understand how a man interprets that glow? That glow says to him, "I not only love you, I admire you. I respect you for who you are. I want to spend the rest of my life feeling this way about you." That glow was there almost every time you were around him. He thought that would last for-ever. After all, you both agreed your relationship was different. Once he became assured of your love, he was overwhelmed by the way you be-lieved in him and wanted to honor him for who he was. You viewed him as your Knight in Shining Armor. You were his cheerleader. "Where you go, I will go!" What set you apart from all other women in his life was that "look," the glowing look that says, "I respect you." You expressed awe over him.

Then in the first year of marriage came a series of fights. Your spirit was crushed. You got mad at him. During the arguments, he observed a new look in your face. A cold look. A look of disgust. The glow left. He did not know how to help you recapture the glow you had for him. It seemed once a month he was the worst human being on the planet.

Though a woman might say the kind of respect we are talking about is foreign to her, she does somehow realize she had a certain glow during courtship. And it was amazing how he treated her. Of course, she attests that she felt admiration toward him because he loved her. Did he, though feel such fond feelings of affection because she admired who he was in his spirit? Did he talk and talk because he felt esteemed by her? Was his way with her loving because her way was esteeming? We're back to the chicken and egg.

If she gives some Respect Talk to this husband, he may re-open. The more good will that is in this man, the more he'll respond. When she speaks these words again, he will be touched and relieved deep in his spirit. There is no greater pain than to live with someone you think has contempt for who you are as a human being. In such moments, love is not enough to a man. His mother loves him. He knows you love him. But do you respect who he is in his spirit?

We will tell you this. If you hold onto the unbiblical idea that "I don't have to show respect because I don't feel any respect for him," then you've missed God's call to be a respectful woman independent of your husband's performance. Even further, if that is your attitude, your husband will feel about you the same way you would feel about him if he went around say-ing, "I don't have to show love because I don't feel any love for her." You can cry unfair all you want. You can claim love is the preeminent virtue.

But as a follower of Christ, you cannot escape what the Bible teaches and you cannot escape what your husband is certain to feel.

We will tell you another thing. Take heed! Do you know how a woman can tempt your husband? It isn't sex. It's flattery: "...the adulteress who flatters with her words" (Proverbs 2:16). Wives have shared with us how sobering this is. Your husband can be craving admiration, like you crave love. An admiring woman can tempt him. You have good reason to weigh what Scripture reports.

Is Your Husband's Love the Key to Your Self Love?

Scripture is straightforward. "Under three things the earth quakes, And under four, it cannot bear up...Under an unloved woman when she gets a husband" (Proverbs 30:21-23). Because this woman had unresolved issues in her soul, the marriage does not solve her love needs. A wife may feel unloved but that has nothing to do with her husband being an unloving man. This is her issue.

> "...comprehend...what is the breadth and length and height and depth, and to know the love of Christ."
> - Ephesians 3:18,19

If your self-image rests on your husband's image of you, then you will be hypersensitive to his disapproval. If you expect him to love you so that you can love yourself, this is equal to him demanding of you to respect him so he can feel self-respect. The tension you feel in your marriage runs deeper than your husband failing to love you. This is about you feeling good about yourself, and putting that responsibility on your husband's shoulders. When your self-identification is wrapped up in your husband's opinion and he does not value you, you feel worthless. This weight should not be placed on your husband.

> "...to the saints...Blessed be the God and Father of our Lord Jesus Christ, who has blessed us with every spiritual blessing in the heavenly places in Christ"
> - Ephesians 1:1,3

You need an older woman in your life to bring perspective (Titus 2:4). You need her encouragement. You also need to study materials that open up your eyes to God's unconditional acceptance of you in Christ. We recommend discussing the following with a godly wise person.

Your self-love is not derived from your husband's love. It can affect it but does not determine it. True self-love is rooted in God's image of you. In other words, God's image of you must be your image of yourself. Since God loves you, you are to love yourself as God does – or at least move in that direction as you mature. You won't attain this. You can, though, experience a greater sense of self-worth as you commit to believing that God declares you have worth to Him. Your husband's view of you should not be the basis of your self-image. God's image should be the foundation. During marital conflict and tension if you do not have a sufficient degree of biblical self-love, then when your husband is unloving you'll be crushed. You'll resent him. He is not making you feel good about yourself. You'll keep crying out, "Love me!" Your whole self-image cannot rest on your husband's estimation of you.

This is why Ephesians 5 follows Ephesians 1! God speaks to you as one among the "Saints." This means you are viewed as perfect in the eyes of God. This is referred to as your position in Christ. You are to value yourself as God values you. If your self-image rests on your husband's image of you, than if he devalues you by failing to love you, he has failed to be the kind of god you expect him to be. You feel threatened and insecure. Eventually, you cease to revere your "god." He has not healed you.

Is your problem with your husband's lack of love or your disbelief in what God says about you? Have you wrongly held your husband responsible for making you feel good about yourself? He isn't God. Christ is God, and his view is what matters. This doesn't mean you will be without struggles. Your partner can hurt you deeply. But in the deepest sense his lack of love does not undermine your deepest self-view. It actually reveals where you derive your self-worth. If you do not value yourself as God values you, your pattern will be that of blaming your husband for failing to love you. The earth will quake.

"My Identification Card"

In God, I have discovered my true and essential identity. I am somebody eternally secure and significant. I am not better than others or worse than others. In Him, I have been chosen and predestined to adoption by the Father. In Him, I have redemption, forgiveness and obtained an inheritance through the Son. In Him, I was sealed with the Holy Spirit. I believe what is written in Ephesians 1:3-14.

Therefore, on this date _____, I choose to trust His view of me and choose to see myself this way. I do not need to seek my primary identity elsewhere. My essential identity is not derived from my intelligence, beauty, abilities, riches or family. If my identity is based on these and I lose them, I lose my identity. If I gain these things, I can gain a superficial identity and live independent of Christ. Though these things can affect my identity, which can be okay, I will no longer allow them to "determine" my foundational identity as a person, otherwise I build my house on sand. I refuse to believe the lie any longer. Today I make a decision to believe what God says in Scripture.

Thus, I _____ sign this "identification card" as a way of reminding me and revealing that I am secure in my position due to who I am in Christ. I am satisfied. In the deepest sense, I will not look to my spouse's love in order to feel good about myself. My self-love is based on Christ's love of me.

I will now do good things. I will not do this in order to gain God's acceptance. I am already accepted in Christ. But like a wife who responds enthusiastically to unconditional love, so I will respond as the Bride of Christ to God's unconditional love. I will do good things not to appease God but to please God.

The Greatest Demonstration of a Wife's Love

Here is the challenge a wife must accept. Because she sees herself as loving, will she recognize the best way to demonstrate her love to her husband? The most effective way to make your husband feel loved is by coming across respectfully during conflict.

The challenge is simple. Will you be motivated to love your husband with respect? If you are as loving as you say you are, are you willing to show your love by coming across more respectfully?

> **"...esteem them very highly in love..."**
> - I Thessalonians 5:13

May we insert an interesting comment? You can best love and respect without a word! There is loudness in quietness. There is preaching in silence. God has created women beautifully and wonderfully to communicate. However, He countered His own creation with a divine word of caution to every wife, instructing her to win her disobedient husband without a word (1 Peter 3:1,2). "Respectful behavior" convicts him. Preaching and nagging may work short-term but close off the spirit long-term. Sarah says, "When I am silent, Emerson hears himself."

In book two we will guide you in doing this. You'll be joyfully amazed.

There's an Ostrich Standing on the Kitchen Table

Something is unaddressed. Like the children's story about the king who wore no clothes and no one dared tell him otherwise, today something very obvious exists but all are hush-hush.

> **"...who suppress the truth in unrighteousness"**
> - Romans 1:18

We are afraid to address the biblical phrase, "weaker vessel." Peter wrote, "You husbands likewise, live with your wives in an understanding way, as with a weaker vessel, since she is a woman; and grant her honor as a fellow heir of the grace of life, so that your prayers may not be hindered" (1 Peter 3:7).

Do some wives react disrespectfully because they see themselves as the more vulnerable and more easily victimized? Do they react disrespectfully because they expect the husband to be able to "take it?" Do they show contempt – a strong measure to motivate change – because they feel their husbands are tougher and thicker? In other words, as Peter describes it, do wives see themselves as the "weaker vessel" and the husband as the stronger sex?

I, Sarah, have shared with Emerson that when I come at him disrespectfully, I expect him to be able to take it. When it comes to my emotions, I see myself as the more vulnerable. Both of us believe this because of Scripture. From a biblical view, wives are clearly reported as the "weaker vessel."

Does a wife feel, but never speak, that her husband is exercising greater emotional power? Does she never mention being the "weaker vessel" (Isaiah 19:16; Jeremiah 51:30)? Is the ostrich on the kitchen table the unspoken feeling in the wife that she is the weaker and he is the stronger? Is this cultural heresy, making one worthy of social stoning? How are we to understand the phrase in 1 Peter 3:7, "a weaker vessel, since she is a woman"?

God's revelation is reporting an important male and female difference. The Bible says, "since she is a woman" she is "a weaker vessel." This is a gender issue. When a wife does not have a husband who lives with her in an understanding way and honors her as a fellow heir, she is the weaker vessel compared to him. The prophet declares she becomes, "a wife forsaken and grieved in spirit... when she is rejected" (Isaiah 54:6).

Our observation is that when a woman loves a man, she weakens. That's not a dirty word. Put it this way; she's like a porcelain vessel and he's a brass vessel. Not lesser, just different. A porcelain vessel is more vulnerable in comparison to a brass vessel. Brass can smash porcelain. Like the children's game rock-scissors-paper, paper can cover the rock, the rock can smash the scissors, and the scissors can cut the paper. There are different functions, strengths and weaknesses in relationship to each other.

A wife is not a weak vessel; she is a weaker vessel. This is a comparative statement, not a qualitative statement. This is restricted between the husband and wife. That porcelain has less worth is a ridiculous assessment. Porcelain can exceed the worth of brass by light years. For instance, in the area of nurturing a woman is unbelievable. In living longer, she wins. However, in defending a nation, brass has incredible strength. When it comes to emotions, men are different. The one who has the least interest can exercise the greatest power. A husband doesn't have as great a need in the subtleties of the emotions in marital romance. Unfortunately, the one who shows the least interest can be the stronger. Because Hitler had no interest in the Jews, he could kill the Jews, but this, obviously, is an extreme analogy. When it comes to emotions in marriage, your husband, generally speaking, has the least interest. He doesn't have a need to enter the daily drama of romance. Wives recognize this, and want to change him. "You don't bring me flowers anymore." On the other hand, when it comes to sex, you have less interest and therefore exercise more control (Proverbs 5:19; Matthew 5:28; 2 Samuel 11:2). Not wrong, just different.

When a wife feels vulnerable in the face of her husband's lesser interest, she can react disrespectfully. This is her way of countering her husband's misused strength.

But here is where things get confusing. What if a wife never tells her husband she feels this way? What if the only message he hears from his wife is, "We're equal?" What if he hears, "Women are better?" In fact, what if he hears, "Women are the stronger sex?" From a contemporary husband's view, then, when a wife becomes very negative, critical and disrespectful, he sees this as overkill. He doesn't discern her vulnerability as being rooted in her feeling weaker. If she communicates that she is equal, better or stronger, then how easy is it for him to interpret her as vulnerable or feeling victimized? To him, she is mad. He will fight back, and fight back hard. "I don't deserve this disrespect." That she is verbally blasting away from hurt and fear goes over his head. He shuts her out to protect himself.

This is why a Christian wife needs to express the fact that she is porcelain and he is brass. Men respond to the damsel in distress, but if women have been conditioned against what is called the Cinderella Complex, she'll never mention the ostrich, and he won't see it for sure.

> "However, in the Lord, neither is woman independent of man, nor is man independent of woman."
> - I Corinthians 11:11

In our marriage, Sarah eventually told me, "I am disrespectful because you're hurting me by your lack of love and you need to change into a more loving man. I feel too vulnerable to your anger and harshness, and looks of disapproval." She and I believed Peter. Once that was clarified, I realized Sarah wasn't trying to berate me but was appealing to my masculine strength. It changed the complexity of the "fight." That motivated me to be less defensive and angry. It allowed me to receive what Dr. John Gottman calls the "negative influence" from a wife. Some wives do not inform their husbands, so the husbands do not allow themselves to be influenced by the negativity. The men fight back out of self-defense. Of course, the wife filters that as further evidence that he is unloving. Craziness then ensues.

Adding to the confusion, in today's marriage, a husband might not believe that his wife really is the weaker vessel. He may have married her because of her independence. Both liked that idea. He didn't want a woman emotionally dependent, and she had convinced herself that as a single woman, she was the independent type. But then she fell in love. Our nineteen-year-old daughter wrote a college paper on love. "I have always wanted love to be easy. I would feel warm and tingly when I heard my guy friends at school say, 'I love you.' I imagined repeatedly in my head just how (my boyfriend in college) would tell me he loved me for the first time. At different times, I have found myself wanting to find my worth in (my boyfriend)." Elizabeth Bugental, in 'On Intimacy and Death,' wrote, 'Sometimes I am tempted simply to hand myself over to that gentle, loving man who is my husband, to make him a kind of god whom I lovingly serve, instead of my equal and partner. Giving myself over to him would be, at least initially, so restful' (p. 182). It's so simple for me to want to become a part of him and leave my individual behind."

Our daughter is very profound. She is a woman, and this is how women feel. She can find her worth in her husband, she can hand herself over, and she can leave her individual behind. That's not hard for a woman in love. But someone tell us, does that not make her vulnerable? Will our daughter not feel weaker for this? When she then feels misunderstood and dishonored, will she not be emotionally crushed? The privilege of womanhood is the capacity to love and feel loved. The curse can be this capacity to love but feel unloved. If our daughter reacts with contempt when hurt, and communicates she is equal if not better, and even stronger, he will not understand. She must talk about the ostrich. This is our counsel to our own daughter. She does not need to be afraid of how God made her, speaking the truth in love, and with respect. Because she feels weaker does not make her weak. God will defend the way He has made her. She need only align herself with Him.

A Wife's Negative Interpretation of this One Word

A wife e-mailed, "I am trying to learn how to respect my husband. He has many respectable qualities. However, his substitution of pornography for intimacy with me has caused a separation. Knowing that this will not be 'cured' overnight, how can I bring myself to show him respect while we try to work things out? I have to rebuild trust all over again."

Emerson replied, "Thanks for sharing your heart with me. This is not easy. You are suffering. Let's begin with a simple yet very important question. When you think of showing respect to your husband what do you think showing respect looks like?" She replied, "Excellent question! I have struggled with this for awhile. I had no respectful (attitude toward male) role models growing up. I respect my boss because he has authority over me. For a husband, when I think of respect, I think of being kind of fake, complimenting him all the time, etc. I need examples, I guess." I asked a second question. What do you want to show or say? She commented, "I want to repair my marriage. I need to boost his self-esteem and help him rise to be the leader of the family. But he isn't, so it seems he hasn't earned it yet." Her reply can literally be heard by millions of women in the West. One, if respect is shown, it is to a superior type. Two, if respect is shown it must be earned.

Scripture does not teach either of these in marriage. Yes, we're to show respect to those in authority because of their authority, and this makes sense. And, yes, we can and do earn respect. But the teaching about respecting a husband is an unconditional respect as we have seen in 1 Peter 3:1,2. Even so, what troubles many wives is the feeling that her husband is living at an inferior level (i.e. pornography) which triggers her feelings of disrespect. Second, he is not living at a higher level (i.e. as a spiritual leader) which turns off any possible response of respect. He is both causing her feelings of disrespect and not causing any feelings of respect. This is the logic wives bring to this topic. Every wife is sincere in these sentiments.

What can a wife do? Peter gives us the clear answer. She must exhibit "respectful behavior" (1 Peter 3:2). In his estimation it has little to do with feeling respect. For instance, how can a wife feel respect for her husband who searches the web for pornography? One cannot FEEL respect. It's about coming across in a respectful manner when confronting him. In a grieved and angry state, a wife can still come across with a respectful demeanor. She does this in obedience to God's command, not because her husband is worthy of it.

In respectfully confronting a husband caught looking at pornography, the call of God to the wife is to carry herself in a dignified manner. She can do one of two things. One, she can scream, "I can't believe how perverted you are.

You're destroying my marriage. You are despicable. You make me vomit. I hope God damns you."

Or, in obedience to God's word, she can enter a spiritual discipline. She can discipline herself to confront his behavior as extremely sinful while speaking respectfully. If Jesus were standing right beside her and said, "Dear, please confront your husband," she would do so truthfully, lovingly and respectfully, perhaps saying, "I am grieved. The temptation of the internet is too great for you. I hate what these pornographers are doing to you. I believe in your spirit, but your flesh is weak, like mine is weak in other areas. You are too honorable of a man in your heart to pursue this. God does not desire this for you and you don't desire this for yourself. What is the honorable thing to do from this point on? I feel like a failure as a wife. This is profoundly threatening to me. I feel unbelievable hurt and anger, but I believe this is your battle, and I believe God is speaking to you about what to do. What will you do? I am your helper. What can I do?"

Easy? It's not a choice in this instance between easy and hard. This is hard either way. The burden is not fair to her, but long term the burden will be less when she confronts her husband respectfully. The days ahead will be a struggle, but the dignified approach has not shamed her husband. If anything it will energize him to pursue a godly course. The other approach will scold him into temporary change. Long term, though, he is apt to be more secretive.

Is such respect possible? Peter had just written that followers of Christ are to show "all respect, not only to those who are good and gentle, but also to those who are unreasonable" (1 Peter 2:18). There are people who are not good, yet we can come across to them in a respectful manner. Respect is something we do, not feel. Respect is something we display from the inside out. Many people miss that. It is about being a respectful wife, not about a husband being respectable. Peter never taught that showing respect was an endorsement of another's evil or harshness or irrationality.

As a follower of Christ, a woman is to carry herself in dignity. We feel that some women have lost the art of walking in dignity in the privacy of their homes. The Bible says, "Women must likewise be dignified" (1 Timothy 3:11). "Strength and dignity are her clothing" (Proverbs 31:25). It may even be that a wife is to see that this issue is more about God and her. One wife introduced a powerful question into her life: "Am I a victim here or is this a Life Lesson from God?" This may not be fair, but it finds favor with God. Peter said so.

1 Peter 2:17   **Honor all men...**

1 Peter 2:18	... with all respect, not only to those who are good and gentle, but also to those who are unreasonable.
1 Peter 2:19	For this finds favor, if for the sake of conscience toward God a man bears up under sorrows when suffering unjustly.
1 Peter 2:20	For what credit is there if, when you sin and are harshly treated, you endure it with patience? But if when you do what is right and suffer for it you patiently endure it, this finds favor with God.
1 Peter 2:21	For you have been called for this purpose, since Christ also suffered for you, leaving you an example for you to follow in His steps,
1 Peter 2:22	who committed no sin, nor was any deceit found in His mouth;
1 Peter 2:23	and while being reviled, He did not revile in return; while suffering, He uttered no threats, but kept entrusting Himself to Him who judges righteously;
1 Peter 3:1	In the same way, you wives...

Peter specifically applied this to wives. As you imitate the example of Christ and entrust yourself to the Father, you find favor with God.

Let's return to the pornography issue. Showing disdain for his spirit absolutely does not work. Yes, lust is sin (Matthew 5:28). That he is visually oriented and more easily enticed should be something you pray about on his behalf. King David watched Bathsheba bathing and was tempted (2 Samuel 11:2). This temptation prompted Job to make a covenant with his eyes (Job 31:1). This is a serious temptation. At the same time, one of the reasons you can come across respectfully is that you too are a sinner. You have different sins but still need the Savior. Sarah has talked with too many women who openly declare, "I am a better person than he is." That's not so, from God's view. Wives may struggle with gluttony, fears, jealousy, gossip, outbursts of anger, and a judgmental spirit, plus women are actually physically abusing males in the home more than men are. Added to this, the worse of all sins might be self-righteousness. Read the story behind Jesus' words: "And He also told this parable to certain ones who trusted in themselves that they were righteous, and viewed others with contempt" (Luke 18:9). Added to this list, depriving your husband sexually can increase his temptation. Satan himself can tempt him (1 Corinthians 7:5). You need to own up to your part here. It is his sin but you can be an accomplice.

Do we want to shame you? Absolutely not, but the key to confronting and correcting a husband is looking at your own propensity to sin. "Brethren, even if a man is caught in any trespass, you who are spiritual, restore such a one in a spirit of gentleness; each one looking to yourself, lest you too be tempted" (Galatians 6:1)

We encourage a wife to prudently think through what, in fact, is happening. She could interpret her husband and the whole marriage through that sinful moment of looking at pornography. That can be a gigantic mistake. God may be calling you to overlook some of this. "Love covers a multitude of sins" (1 Peter 4:8). In addition, that moment does not represent your husband's heart. At other times your husband may be seeking God, sharing his faith, doing Bible study, and caring for others. Remember, the disciples failed Jesus at the lowest point in His life, but He still honored their spirit though their flesh was weak. He did not shame them while confronting them. The Bible says, "In wrath remember mercy" (Habukkuk 3:2). The more disrespectful a wife is perhaps the more self-righteous she has become. Oh, don't get us wrong. We understand your pain, but the way out of this pain is the course Peter establishes. To walk that course, these issues need to be humbly considered.

Honest Questions About Your Feelings as a Woman

"...Now this time my husband will become attached to me..."
- Genesis 29:34

"Look, all of this is unfair to me. I want to love and be loved. If that happens, we'll all be happy. If I don't feel loved, he needs to change. I don't like all this talk about respect. It's too foreign. My husband isn't into gross sins, so can't we return to my way of thinking? Love is all that matters." This is pink speaking. Again, God created us male and female, not female and female! It's too easy, and unwise, for a wife to assume that because she is motivated by love then her husband should be motivated in exactly the same way. For example, she moves toward him to talk, giving the report of her day in order to build rapport. She then expects him to give the report of his day to build rapport with her. But, when it's his turn to talk, he says very little. So she asks, "Well, how was your day?" He replies, "Fine." She asks, "Anything happen of interest?" He says, "No, it was the same as it is every day. What's for dinner?" Not only, then, does her desire to increase the feeling of love between them not work, she actually feels the love drain away.

So, what can a wife do? In book two we set forth many practical things she can do that will bring about mutual satisfaction. On this point, we highlight the difference between face-to-face talking and shoulder-to-shoulder activities. Sometimes the best way to engage a husband to talk is by not trying to talk to him directly. We explain in book two what we mean.

"Well, why am I as a wife expected to act on this? My husband has the primary responsibility to initiate, right?" Yes and no. The one who sees himself or herself as the most mature should move first. Do you see yourself as more mature? You go first. Also, this book is written to you, not your husband, so we're challenging you. Peter wrote to women. The apostles did not see wives as passive responders. The Energizing Cycle declares: her respect motivates his love. A wife can bring about change in the marriage when she acts on this principle. Of course every wife wants to be loved first. That is understandable and right. But God is not focusing on your rights. He is focusing on your call. You have a call to impact your marriage His way. God's Word works.

Ephesians 5:33   **Nevertheless let each individual among you also love his own wife even as himself; and let the wife see to it that she respect her husband.**

1 Peter 3:1, 2   **your... husbands ...even if any of them are disobedient to the word, they may be won without a word by the behavior of their wives, as they observe your... respectful behavior.**

"where is...honor? ...where is...respect."
- Malachi 1:6,8

"And the contentions of a wife are a constant dripping."
- Proverbs 19:13

"Are you saying I should never love my husband?" He needs your love, and is motivated by love! Love is still needed. God designed you to love and expects you to love. But God, through Paul and Peter, is revealing that the most powerful way to motivate your husband is through respect.

"Are you saying my disrespect is causing him to lose motivation to love me?" Well, yes – it certainly can! Remember how the Crazy Cycle goes: without respect, a husband reacts without love. Ostensibly, if a wife is disrespectful one day and then loving the next, she is working against herself. As we discussed earlier, her loving efforts are offset by disrespect. He is motivated by her love, but is even more de-motivated by what appears to him as her contentious and contemptuous spirit. By way of comparison, what do you feel if your husband respects you a lot (i.e. honors you with the purchase of a new home) but every six months he harshly screams, "I don't love you!"? His lack of love outweighs his respect. In your case, if you love him all year long but one day shout, "I don't respect you! I never have and never will!" you counteract your love. In book two, we tell you how to rebound from this if you have done this.

> **"...who flatters with her words."**
> - Proverbs 7:5

We said earlier that every man does what he does for the admiration of one woman, and you are that woman. If over time he feels you no longer admire him, even though you love him, he no longer has that unique woman in his life. She's gone. This is why he is vulnerable to another woman's flattery.

We understand your feelings as a wife. Do you understand what your husband feels? Yes, your husband needs to understand you, too; we want that for you. We happen to believe that the best way for you to be understood is to seek to understand your husband. Said another way, **understand to be understood**. Let's gain additional insight into your husband.

INSIGHTS Into a Husband

Husbands Want to Love and Please Their Wives

Husbands want to love. "So Jacob served seven years for Rachel and they seemed to him but a few days because of his love for her" (Genesis 29:20). Men fall in love, and it is a wonderful thing to observe, as Solomon did. "There are three things which are too wonderful for me, Four which I do not understand" and he then sights the fourth as "the way of a man with a maid" (Proverbs 30:18,19). Husbands do not want to displease their wives. Paul writes, "but one who is married is concerned about the things of the world, how he may please his wife" (1 Corinthians 7:33).

So why do some wives not feel this way? Given the husbands have good will, why are some wives so critical in their spirits toward their men? Maybe there is a huge misunderstanding of men. Men react in ways that wives are absolutely convinced are unloving, and thus point toward him as uncaring. Martha even did this toward Jesus. She had the audacity to confront Jesus as uncaring: "But Martha was distracted with all her preparations; and she came up to Him, and said, "Lord, do You not care that my sister has left me to do all the serving alone? Then tell her to help me" (Luke 10:40). Some men, even the Son of God himself, can act and react in ways that women can misread. Take, for example, the stories we've shared about when husbands react unlovingly when feeling disrespected. He gets angry and goes silent, closing you out. To you, that shouts, "I don't love you." But that's not his message at all. His message is, "I feel disrespected by you. I don't deserve this. So, I am going to do the honorable thing and be quiet so this doesn't get out of control. I feel you are provoking me. Somebody needs to protect this marriage." That's what he feels. Through pink lenses though, that makes very little sense. You don't deal with intimate relationships like this. Since women are often described as the evaluators of truth in a relationship, these husbands come out looking very bad. The fact is, many times the man seeks to do the respectful thing – and even the loving thing – by going silent! Boy, do we have a failure to communicate here, or what?

Do You Really Want to Know?

Would you be absolutely honest for a moment on one point? If your husband felt something very strongly which you did not feel – and if that feeling explained much of why he acted the way he did – would you really want to know about it? Or would you simply dismiss the feeling, thinking about your own feelings instead? That's human nature, of course, to validate our own feelings and dismiss anyone else's that might disagree with our own. But this is about understanding your husband to help him understand you; it's not about validating his concerns over yours. That's very important to think about. This is to benefit you and the marriage, not to give

> "The woman of folly is boisterous, She is naive, and knows nothing."
> - Proverbs 9:13

him carte blanche to act unlovingly. But you have to be willing to step out in faith on this.

Let's ask a few more questions.

> "My people are destroyed for lack of knowledge...you have rejected knowledge...Since you have forgotten the law of your God, I also will forget your children." -Hosea 4:6

1. If you unintentionally reacted in ways that resulted in your husband losing motivation to show his love, would you want to know what you were unintentionally doing and stop that? If God revealed what to do, would you want to know this?

2. If your husband reacted to you by getting angry, expressing disrespect, going quiet and/or walking away, would you be open to discovering that this may have very little to do with him not loving you, even though this screams, "I don't love you!"? If God revealed what to do in response, would you want to know this?

3. If you felt that because you loved your husband he had no right to feel disrespected, yet he was feeling disrespected and losing motivation to

show you more love, would you want to know about his feelings and what to do about those feelings?

As we've done conferences, we realized how sobering this material is to some wives. Women are wonderful, and yet we continue to have a growing suspicion that in the culture in which we live an unwritten license has been given to wives to be negative, critical and disrespectful toward their husbands. Women have gotten the signal that it's okay to be disrespectful, and out of their deep frustrations with things they tend to choose this method time and time again to motivate the husband to be more loving or to punish him for being unloving. And it backfires and backfires and backfires.

> **"Every man's way is right in his own eyes, But the Lord weighs the hearts."**
> - Proverbs 21:2

In our observation, here's how many wives process the issue of their disrespect. First, a wife feels she is far more loving in the relationship, so she rationalizes the issue of her disrespect, thinking that in the bigger scheme it's not the real issue. Besides, he should be man enough to take it. Second, a husband needs to change his unloving manner far more than she needs to change her disrespectful demeanor. Love is the higher virtue, and she is the better lover. He needs to change first and more. Third, because love is the greatest and he needs to be more loving, if she is disrespectful to change him,

> **"But He answered and said, 'It is written, 'Man shall not live on bread alone, but on every word that proceeds out of the mouth of God.'"** - Matthew 4:4

that is the loving thing to do! Disrespect can be the means used to achieve a worthy end. Besides, if he doesn't respond to her love, what other alternative is there? Fourth, if she is disrespectful in order to make him loving, this is more justified than if he is unloving to make her respectful. In her mind, her disrespect to motivate love can be virtuous. His lack of love to motivate her respect is vile.

> **"For the wisdom of this world is foolishness before God...'The Lord knows the reasonings of the wise, that they are useless."**
> - I Corinthians 3:19, 20

Each wife has to decide if the Bible is her guide. Is Scripture the final authority for her faith and practice? How we long for wives to trust this

Bible verse as it relates to respect: "And for this reason we also constantly thank God that when you received from us the word of God's message, you accepted it not as the word of men, but for what it really is, the word of God, which also performs its work in you who believe" (1 Thessalonians 2:13). Voices will say that Paul and Peter are men. As men they are clueless about what women feel and don't understand how to change a husband.

> **"that you should remember the words spoken beforehand by the holy prophets and the commandment of the Lord and Savior spoken by your apostles."**
>
> *- 2 Peter 3:2*

Showing respect is absurd. If a wife does not feel respect, her husband does not deserve respect. If her husband does not deserve respect, she does not have to feel respect nor show respect.

What you are up against are your feelings. The call of God is to exercise faith in the facts of Scripture above feelings that run contrary to Scripture. It isn't easy but it is godly, and God's heart is touched when you do it.

A Word About Motivation and a Word about Conflict

Let me, Emerson, say a word about motivation. When I know what Sarah needs, I can know how to motivate Sarah. Since Sarah's deepest need is to feel my love, that's the key to motivating her. If my deepest need is to feel respected – given that I am assured of her love – then that's the key to motivating me. Motivation is simple: find out what a person needs, seek to meet that need, and watch the positive response. Refuse to respond to that need and watch that person negatively react. Show disrespect toward a husband and observe him get angry, speak disrespectfully, go quiet and walk away. It's almost like a law of physics, really.

And a corollary to that "law," if you will, is that when you motivate another person by meeting his need, he tends to respond by meeting your need. Jesus said, "And just as you want people to treat you, treat them in the same way" (Luke 6:31). Since Jesus said it, it works. But in marriages these days, most wives try to love their husbands in order for their husbands to love them. Their thinking is: "I need love and my husband needs love, so I'll love him which will motivate him to love me." That sounds like the Golden Rule, but it is really the woman's romantic rule. It should

be, "I need love and my husband needs respect,   **"and let us consider**
according to Scripture, so I'll treat him with re-   **how to stimulate one**
spect to motivate him to treat me with love." There   **another to love..."**
  - Hebrews 10:25
is no guarantee on this, but most good-willed husbands respond exactly this way, especially over time.

This does not mean that if you begin practicing this that all conflict will suddenly halt. The larger truth is that God intends for some conflict to exist in a marriage. Read these two verses: "The wife does not have authority over her own body, but the husband does; and likewise also the husband does not have authority over his own body, but the wife does" (1 Corinthians 7:4). And, "be subject to one another in the fear of Christ" (Ephesians 5:21). Clearly the Lord intends for a measure of tension to exist in every marriage. Who has authority over whom? Who is to submit to whom? The answer to both questions is: yes! In other words, God intends for couples to experience stress, and from that create a "win-win" situation when conflict occurs. God is not surprised by couples who have strong opposing feelings. He designed it this way! What grieves Him is when a husband truly reacts unlovingly and a wife truly reacts disrespectfully in direct disobedience to His revelation.

For example, the husband feels he has the authority to decide they should be sexually intimate tonight. The wife feels she has right to decide that they will not be sexually intimate tonight. Or, he expects his wife to defer to his sexual desires and she expects him to yield to her lack of sexual desire. God's Word reveals in certain settings that two individuals will need to create a compromise of some kind. He submits to her authority this time round. She submits to his authority next time around. What saddens the Lord is the ensuing hate and contempt because of the conflict. She screams, "I think you're despicable for wanting sex." He yells, "You are so frigid you'd freeze a glass of water." That's the problem, not the fact that there is conflict to begin with. The conflict is human, but the response can strengthen the marriage and please God, or it can erode the marriage and grieve God. It's how we deal with it that concerns Him.

Successful couples enter conflict, which is not a happy experience, with their eye on coming up with loving and respectful ways to create a "win-win" situation, as we phrase it. They do not freak out when there is conflict that demands one defers to what the other prefers. They do not conclude, "We must not be meant for one another." To them, that's ridiculous. They know that God has joined them together; they are husband and wife. Conflicts are part and parcel of marriage. They maturely accept a degree of clashing! We – Emerson and Sarah – have some tension on a regular basis. Praise the Lord, we're human. Should we buy a car for our daughter, should we urge our son to pursue a job, should we buy some furniture, should we move the furniture in the liv-

> "But if you should marry, you have not sinned...Yet such will have trouble in this life, and I am trying to spare you."
> - I Corinthians 7:28

ing room, should we eat at this time or that time, did you call so and so, did you hear what I said, did you clean up the kitchen, etc? All in one day! As Ruth Graham used to say, "If Billy and I agreed on everything one of us would be unnecessary!"

Know then, that the presence of conflict does not mean you have a bad marriage, or a marriage that wasn't meant to be in the first place. That is a powerful lie in our culture and we need to know that it is a lie, that God is not in it, that He hates it, and that if you believe it you will never be able to successfully deal with the conflicts in your relationship. The difference between couples

> "What therefore God has joined together, let no man separate."
> - Mark 10:9

with great marriages and those with bad marriages is *not* the absence of conflict. It is the ability to decode why the other is negatively reacting and to know what to do to increase the positive feelings between them. As a wife, these pages are about you discovering ways to influence your husband and to increase the positive feelings of love in the marriage. Don't panic if there is conflict. Instead, see conflict as God's opportunity for you to convince and convict your husband God's way!

What Convicts a Husband

We firmly believe every husband is convicted by a wife's unconditional respect. This is God's revelation to Peter (1 Peter 3:1,2) and God will honor His own instruction. Those husbands who have sinned against their wives, God will convict. Malachi declared, "...the Lord has been a witness between you and the wife of your youth, against whom you have dealt treacherously." (Malachi 2:14). A wife who follows Jesus must take this by faith. As she does the respecting, God does the shaming. Only the believing wife will trust in this. The Christ-Follower will believe in the convicting power of God's Spirit (John 16:8).

If a wife seeks to be respectful when pointing out that she is hurt, her husband will not ignore her hurt – certainly not long term, if her husband is a good-willed man who is sincerely following Christ. Her honor convicts him and motivates him to make amends. You see, often a husband negatively reacts to his wife, not because she points out his unloving tendencies, but because of his feeling that she does not respect him because of those unloving tendencies! Don't forget, it's the issue behind the issue. When she approaches him respectfully, he'll seek reconciliation. A wife needs to pay more attention to how a husband makes amends. It isn't always the way she might expect. A husband may be convicted and be apologizing, but a wife might not even see it because he isn't doing it her way.

> "and keep a good conscience so that in the thing in which you are slandered, those who revile your good behavior in Christ may be put to shame." - I Peter 3:16

Here's an example of what we mean. A wife was having marital tension. She acted on what we suggested and told us about it. "I did write him an e-mail, using some of your suggestions, and he never said anything about it, but he's been much more loving lately. Shortly after the conference, he even suggested that the entire family go out for supper, which he has *never* done before, and we had a wonderful time..."

Notice that she said, "he never said anything about it." A wife wants words of love spoken to her. She wants to hear, "I'm sorry," or "I love you." Yet look at the power of her respect! She said, "he's been much more loving lately." Wow! He took the family out to dinner, which he had never done before. And they had a wonderful time. Still, she was looking for him to say some-

> "let us not love with word or with tongue, but in deed and truth." - I John 3:18

thing about her e-mail, and we sensed a measure of disappointment, a feeling that she had to settle for the lesser good. We are always amazed at the level of disappointment in wives who readily admit their husbands have responded in extraordinary ways but who have not responded in the romantic way she would if the situation was reversed. Eve had Paradise but she wanted more.

Often husbands are under conviction and are attempting to rectify things, but their wives don't see it or accept it because it isn't happening exactly the way they want. When Sarah acts this way, I definitely feel convicted. But do I tell her? Rarely, but her respect is working, and working big time. In your husband's case, he may not use words like, "I am sorry." He should – and let's hope eventually he will – but at this point he may not. Somehow though, he'll try to make restitution with an action. Watch for it. Don't overlook what he does. In the male world it is clear as crystal. To him – in his code – he is shouting, "I'm sorry!" He is under conviction and is trying to make things right.

Among men, making amends can be obvious. He's been doing this with his male friends for years. For example, Bob borrows his best friend's baseball glove. But Bob's dog finds it, and eats half of it. Going to his best friend he says, "Joe, I feel horrible. I'll replace it, though I know there's not another glove like it. I am really sorry." Joe shouts angrily, "Bob, where is your brain? I can't believe this. You're so stupid. I knew you'd do something dumb like this. Whenever I give you stuff, you ruin it." Joe leaves the room in a huff. Bob sits in the living room staring out the window. Fifteen minutes later, he goes to where Joe is and says again respectfully, "I really am sorry. I'm depressed. I wanted to kill my dog. I knew how much that glove meant to you. You have plenty of reason to be mad." Bob goes back to the living room. A half hour later, Joe comes into the room and says, "The Yankees are playing, why don't you turn on the TV? I'm getting a coke. Want one?"

Every man knows this is Joe's way of saying it's over with. He's moving on, making amends and dropping the issue. He knows Bob didn't do it on purpose, and Bob has sought to honor him. Few women can grasp this. Most exclaim, "If you don't talk about it, there will never be resolution." Trust me ladies, Joe was upset over the loss of his glove, but he was also under conviction for what he said to his friend. He didn't verbally apologize, and maybe he should have, but then again, it was crystal clear to Bob that Joe was making amends. What Joe was "saying" was obvious to

Bob. Having Bob turn on the Yankee game screamed, "Bob, I accept your apology. Let's move on. It's over with. Let's resume the friendship."

We read the above story between Bob and Joe to our son, Jonathan, who's in his mid-20's. We asked him what Joe was doing. He thought this was some kind of joke. "It's obvious. He was saying, 'We're friends again.'" We asked our other son, David, also in his 20's, what's going on? "Joe forgave him." If as a wife, you wrong your husband and respectfully apologize, yet he is harsh with you, keep your distance in dignity and watch what happens. If he does not directly say, "I am sorry," he'll make amends somewhere. Look for it. If you have done nothing wrong, yet he

> "But if your enemy is hungry, feed him, and if he is thirsty, give him a drink; for in so doing you will heap burning coals upon his head." -Romans 12:20

is angry about something, and you respond respectfully as you describe your hurt, he'll make amends at some future point! If he is a good-willed man, it is inevitable. In either case, look for it through blue lenses. Your respect will convict and motivate him. Respect heaps burning coals on his head. But you have to look for his response outside your feminine standards.

We appeal to you to do that which convicts your husband. Peter is clear: respectful behavior wins a husband. In other words, unconditional respect allows God to act. It's God's way of getting the job done and it works. Respectful behavior does something to a man's spirit, and he stops mistreating you. Let go of some of your womanly expectations as to what that looks like. Look for him to serve you, but let it be his way. When you read book two, **Motivating Your Man God's Way: Applying One Word that Energizes Him to Love**, we will step you through this in practical ways.

At First He May Not Understand His Own Feelings

Husbands intuitively get the respect issue, but they often guard their feelings because it isn't culturally acceptable to feel this way. Some suppress the very idea of it. They develop the bad habit of blaming their negative reactions on other things. If you ask your husband, "Are you feeling

> **"For the queen's conduct will become known to all the women causing them to look with contempt on their husbands."**
> - Esther 1:17

disrespected right now?" he may say, "No." One reason he'll say "no" is out of fear you might follow that question up with a criticism, "Well, that's ridiculous and haughty." Or, he may not be in tune with why he feels as he does. He has been pounded into thinking that he doesn't deserve respect unless he is loving, and he certainly hasn't heard about unconditional respect. He lives it but has not put a voice and vocabulary to this. Why allow this to continue? Let's be mature and get to the real issues underneath the negative reactions. You need to give him the freedom to discover things about himself. As you move into book two, some of you will see your husband get in touch with his inner person. It can be a life-changing experience for him. For the first time, he decodes why he negatively reacts. This enables him to correct this knee jerk reaction. The beautiful thing is that even if a husband is not fully aware of his inner needs, when a wife acts on this, she will observe him respond very positively to her. It is a law of romance. Her respect motivates him to be a loving person. He won't know what hit him!

When you get into a discussion with your husband about his need for respect, be prepared for him to tell you that you are disrespectful. However, don't read into that. That may not be a criticism as much as a testimony of his self-discovery. We'll explain more in book two.

Husbands Wear Blue Hearing Aids, Not Pink Hearing Aids!

When you cry out for love with negative, verbal criticism: "I need you to love me!" he doesn't always hear that. Instead he hears in the negativity, "I don't respect you, Bozo, unless you change right now." As we've indicated, Blue doesn't hear with his blue hearing aids what Pink is saying. Her negative reactions and words distort the deeper message of her heart. We seek to help wives more accurately represent their hearts. Otherwise husbands tend to misinterpret them.

> **"He created them male and female."**
> - Genesis 5:2

The classic illustration is Rachel and Jacob. The love between them was unprecedented. "So Jacob served seven years for Rachel and they

seemed to him but a few days because of his love for her" (Genesis 29:20).
But as in all marriages, a burden arose. Rachel was grieving and upset over
her barrenness. She vented: "Now when Rachel saw that she bore Jacob
no children, she became jealous of her sister; and she said to Jacob, 'Give
me children, or else I die'" (Genesis 30:1). Did Jacob hear her deeper cry
for reassurance and love? No, he felt disrespected. He felt an unrealistic
expectation was being placed on him. "Then Jacob's anger burned against
Rachel, and he said, 'Am I in the place of God, who has withheld from you
the fruit of the womb?'" (Genesis 30:2). Jacob processed her cry through
his blue hearing aids.

Please pay attention to the male! Ask a man, "Do you want your asso-
ciates to love you or respect you?" Watch that man and the men around
him chuckle. He'll say, "I could care less if they loved me, but respect me:
absolutely." Being respected isn't an ego thing any more than being loved
is an ego thing to a woman. God has made your husband a male. This is a
need. We've heard men say, "I don't know how to say this without it
coming across wrong, but I'd rather have a wife respect me than love me."
Even though he needs love and would say he needs love, the thing that
distresses him the most is contempt. There are many people in his world
who do not love him. But to have people not respect him, that is gigantic in
the male arena. Though both love and respect are desired by all of us, there
is something very important to a man about being respected for who he is
deep inside of him as a human being. It is in his wiring. Don't condemn
this, work with it. Paul and Peter were illumined by God to reveal this to
protect wives from making a huge mistake, albeit an innocent one.

Why Husbands Withdraw and Go Silent

Have you heard your husband say, "You
aren't respecting me," and then pull back from
you? Or, "You need to show me more respect,"
and then go quiet? Or, "I don't deserve this disrespect" and walk away? Or, "Everybody respects me but you," and block you out? If so,
please listen. If you've ever said, "I love you but don't respect you," please

"It is better to live in a corner of a roof, Than in a house shared with a contentious woman"
- Proverbs 21:9

listen. That is comparable to him saying, "I respect you but don't love you." One wife said, "If I respect him in fifty areas, but disrespect him in one area, I don't feel any respect for him at all."

(Which is irrational to a man.) If that describes you, please listen. That is equal to him saying, "If there were fifty things I loved about her, but one thing I did not love about her, then I would feel no love for her in my heart." If a husband said that, wives would want to lynch him.

Want to bring him out of his shell? Try this. The next time you apologize to him, do it differently and watch what happens. Typically, when you say I am sorry, you are apologizing for what you feel is your unloving reactions. But is that

an accurate apology? He knows you love him, and does not see you as unloving. He sees himself as the more unloving, as do you. So, does he really believe you need to say, "I am sorry for being unloving?" Probably not. (Actually, he can see that as manipulation to get him to apologize.) But we can tell you what he does feel. He feels you were disrespectful. What if you said, "I am sorry for being disrespectful. You didn't deserve for me to say those things to you. That was too dishonoring." Watch what happens. You are using "respect" words. Our prediction is that you'll see a whole different look in his eyes, and you'll sense something come over him toward you. You might even observe him feel those fond feelings of love!

Does Your Husband Have Good Will?

In writing all this, we are assuming your husband has basic good will. If your husband has evil will, and is doing evil, you need to seek counsel. Such evil-willed men exist. We've met them and the Bible describes them. Paul says in 1 Corinthians 7:11 that there are times when it is wise for a wife to physically "leave" her husband. (If she does leave, the Bible says, she must remain unmarried or be reconciled, given there is no adultery and desertion). Husbands can act in sin. Let us be emphatically clear that our frame of reference in all of these discussions is one in which PHYSICAL

ABUSE IS ABSENT. We are assuming your husband has basic good will. Please be cautious, however, in labeling him as abusive if there is no physical abuse. We have had many women tell us their husbands were abusing them. We envisioned physical abuse. We soon realized that the majority of those women were referring to the husbands' silent treatment. They were not talking to the wives! They were stonewalling. Because that felt so unloving, the women felt free to label that as abuse. But these good willed husbands were wrongly labeled as abusive because they were angry and withdrawn. They were wrongly branded as unloving. The reality can be that the men are seeking to "please" their wives (1 Corinthians 7:33). The men's negative reaction is to the wives' disrespect. Though it comes across as unloving, it is rooted in the men's intentions to do the honorable thing. The husbands are trying to calm themselves down to protect the wives and the marriage. That is not abuse. Because the women's emotional need to talk is unmet does not allow them to claim the men are abusive.

> **"do not go on passing judgment before the time, but wait until the Lord comes who will... disclose the motives of men's hearts."**
> - I Corinthians 4:5

A wife wrote her appreciation concerning the challenge we extended to see the good will in her spouse: "You made the point that most of the time our mates hurt us out of ignorance. You got us to look beyond the offense to the good motive that stimulated it. How hurtful it is to be slammed for something you did with good intentions. Your stories illustrated that he meant well. ...Being flawed, they often go about it in the wrong ways, which feel unloving, but when I look beyond the flawed efforts to the good intentions behind them, it changes my whole attitude. He means well. We are charmed when our children bring us wilted wildflowers because we see the love behind the scrunched up blossoms. We need to look at our mate's efforts the same way."

That says it pretty well. A wife needs to exercise godly discernment. Her husband may not be who she wants him to be but is he deserving of contempt? One way that you may be able to significantly soften your negative feelings toward your husband is by reminding yourself of his good will.

Is Your Husband Failing to Be Who You Want Him to Be?

We should also be very clear in our discussion that the kind of respect we mean has nothing to do with domination or subservience. It is simply respect for your husband as one created in the Image of God. Just as you need to be loved for who you are as a woman, so your man needs to feel you respect him for who he is as a man. If

> "Then the Lord answered Job... Behold, your expectation is false."
> - Job 40:6; 41:9

your husband only loves you if you perform at a certain level, you will feel hurt and unmotivated. If you only respect your husband if he performs according to a standard created by you, he will feel the same way.

Michal came to a point where she saw David as something she did not want him to be. In her opinion, he danced as a fool before the people. David and his actions, though, were acceptable to God. David was not wrong. How sad that Michal despised him. She was wrong but didn't see it (2 Samuel 6:20).

In her book, **Beloved Unbeliever**, Jo Berry writes, "Diane confessed...she mentally put down her husband. She mocked his ideas and his reactions or responses and secretly made fun of his opinions... One day, when she visited him at his office, she was struck by the tremendous respect his co-workers, his secretary and his boss showed him. She shared how she got a knot in her stomach when she heard a man who is older and more experienced than her husband say, 'Yes, sir,' to him. And she was both frightened and ashamed when she saw how his young secretary looked up to and admired him... 'When I got to the car, I started crying... The thing that disturbed me most is that I was judging him not because of his actions or because he isn't a good husband, but because he wasn't what I wanted him to be...'" (p.48).

What do you feel about the insights concerning your husband? Is God requesting you to follow His path to your husband's heart? We believe your faith can motivate you to do what's right, even though your feelings might tell you otherwise.

Let's consider your faith.

FEELINGS and Faith

The Peter Principle: It Isn't What You Think

In business, the Peter Principle is when a person gets promoted beyond his/her competency. Well, that isn't what we mean by the Peter Principle. Peter's principle in our context is: if a wife shows unconditional respect she can win her husband. Many wives will say, "He doesn't deserve my respect." Our response is, that is correct on many fronts. This is why Peter teaches wives to show unconditional respect: "wives...if any of them are disobedient to the word, they may be won...as they observe your...respectful behavior (1 Peter 3:1,2). In the context of this Scripture, Peter taught that the follower of Christ is to be respectful even toward those who don't deserve respect. Again, look at 1 Peter 2:18, "respect...not only... those who are good and gentle, but also... those who are unreasonable." That is unconditional respect! That too is the meaning of the phrase, "Honor all men" (1 Peter 2:17). Respectful behavior is so mighty it can win a disobedient husband back to Christ. He can open his spirit up to God because of his wife's respect. Talk about empowering women! Paul too sees women as having power (1 Corinthians 7:11,16). When a man opens his heart to God, he'll open his soul to his wife. This is why we say a husband is motivated by respect. Both his feelings for God and his wife can change. This is truly amazing, and apart from God's revelation, how many wives would conclude this? A wife's respectful tones and facial expressions motivate her husband beyond any-

> "For how do you know, O wife, whether you will save your husband?"
> - I Corinthians 7:16

> "let her... be reconciled to her husband."
> - I Corinthians 7:11

> "Women must likewise be dignified." - I Timothy 3:11

thing she would have imagined on her own. She can actually win her husband to God without saying a thing! Her respectful behavior alone has immeasurable convicting power. What godly wise wife today believes this? Do we have a crisis of marriage or do we have a crisis of faith? Something to think about.

When a wife makes a decision to adorn herself with dignity, a husband can literally change his emotional responses overnight. Peter knew this – or to be more accurate, God knew this and communicated it to us through Peter. This is why Peter speaks to wives about their outer adornment: "And let not your adornment be merely external – braiding the hair, and wearing gold jewelry, or putting on dresses; but let it be the hidden person of the heart, with the imperishable quality of a gentle and quiet spirit, which is precious in the sight of God. For in this way in former times the holy women also, who hoped in God, used to adorn themselves..." (1 Peter 3:3-5). Where is your heart? Do you have a gentle spirit in response to your husband's weaknesses? Do you have a quiet spirit when your husband is disobedient? Those who know you, would they say you adorn yourself in a style that is respectful?

What some wives find challenging is the emotional dimension of their lives. On the one hand, we defend the negative influence a wife brings to her husband. He needs to receive more of this. But is anyone inviting wives to take their personal lives to a higher level on this topic of unconditional respect? There is a sinful line over which a wife can step and should not. Certain negative, emotional reactions that come across as contemptuous can be as sinful as a husband who comes across angry. We are calling godly, wise women, who themselves are full of good will, to take the respect challenge set forth in the Bible. Who is informing you to consider the respect side of the equation? Who is instructing you to make this a major investment of your energy? Who is appealing to you to act on God's Word in this area? We happen to think that one chief reason wives are not doing this is that few teachers and counselors have developed this teaching to any depth. No one is really extending this call from God. If the wives are left in the dark on this, how loving is that? We choose to assume that most godly, wise wives want to know this because they love Jesus and His Word. These women are not rebelling; they are uninformed.

Even so, there is bound to be someone who screams, "Oh, move into the 21st Century! We are way beyond what was written 2000 years ago. Besides, there is no way I am going to bow to my husband as though he is some god." Peter isn't asking you to bow to anybody but Jesus Christ. He had just written, Jesus is the One who "bore our sins in His body on the cross," not your husband. (1 Peter 2:24). Jesus is "the Shepherd and Guardian of your souls," not your husband (1 Peter 2:25). Peter knew the difference between

> "And Elijah came near to all the people and said, 'How long will you hesitate between two opinions? If the Lord is God, follow Him but if Baal, follow him.' But the people did not answer him a word."
> - I Kings 18:21

majesty and man. Please don't let your quick lips get ahead of Scripture. Paul warned, "learn not to exceed what is written, in order that no one of you might become arrogant..." (1 Corinthians 4:6). Anyone who has the attitude that says, we are much more sophisticated than what the Bible says here, needs to hear the Apostle John: "Anyone who goes too far and does not abide in the teaching of Christ, does not have God; the one who abides in the teaching, he has both the Father and the Son" (2 John 1:9).

Peter's teaching is not antiquated or insufficient. Because words are easy for a wife to use, she needs to be cautious with flippancy. As for the 21st Century, it is most germane. Disrespect toward men is at an all time high. Husbands may not deserve respect, but they don't deserve disrespect either.

Some wives have crossed the line in a way that women in other cultures have not. Is this liberation or destruction? One wife wrote me, "Remember me? I'm the one with all the Harvard degrees who had never heard of the concept of unconditional respect. Your message has had a profound, positive impact on our marriage... I have tried to understand the meaning of unconditional respect and to really respect (my husband). I've had the opportunity to observe in

> "...regard...as worthy of all honor so that the name of God and our doctrine may not be spoken against. And...not be disrespectful...Teach and preach these principles."
> - I Timothy 6:1, 2

other couples the destructiveness of the wife's lack of respect. I believe that you're onto something huge here...what is really revolutionary in your message is the concept of unconditional respect... The respect message itself is really gender neutral: We both owe each other unconditional respect, it's just that the men give it more easily and need it more... It seems that in the old 'woman, obey me' context the women often were treated with neither love nor respect. Now our society has swung in the opposite direction to a love-dominated marriage model and the men are suffering the most..."

Perhaps Peter is more relevant in the 21st Century than in any other time in history. The rightful gains of the feminist movement – women's liberation – do not warrant women dishonoring other human beings. That does not constitute freedom. Peter could not have been clearer: "Act as free men, and do not use your freedom as a covering for evil, but use it as bondslaves of God" (1 Peter 2:16). Where the movement has promoted justice, we applaud it. Where it has promoted contempt toward men, that is evil. Women have no biblical right to do this anymore than men do toward women. We are both created in the Image of God. God is not Pink. God is not Blue. He is both pink and blue, or purple, shall we say. Together we reflect God's image. One is not better than the other, one is different from the other; insofar as basic gender. Thus, unconditional respect is a God-given principle intended for the benefit of all His creatures, and as such it needs to be taught and preached. As wives need unconditional love, husbands need unconditional respect. We believe this is the answer in the 21st Century. Far from being archaic, maybe the Word of Jeremiah needs to be heard: "Thus says the Lord, 'Stand by the ways and see and ask for the ancient paths, Where the good way is, and walk in it; And you shall find rest for your souls.' But they said, 'We will not walk in it.' (Jeremiah 6:16).

What If You Don't "Feel" Right About This?

The struggle you will have now is with how alien all of this is. It doesn't feel right. For example, during romance, you might naturally say, "I am lovesick."

> **"I am lovesick."**
> - Solomon 2:5

To hear your husband say, "I am respect-sick" would sound a little sick! As a woman, you don't feel respect in the way that you feel love, and so you don't naturally desire to show respect in the way that you naturally desire to show love. Because of this, suspicion exists; surely this respect nonsense cannot be right. Maybe you find yourself relating to one wife's comments to us: "When you give the examples from both the husband and the wife's views, they are VERY helpful. I am still amazed, though, how I can read your example of the husband loving the wife and COMPLETELY identify. However, when I read the example of the wife respecting her husband, I have to take it at face value, as my pink sunglasses would not have come to the correct conclusion. I cannot see on my own the husband's motivation or reaction from the respect position. Will this always seem so foreign? I am utterly amazed at how clueless I am at some of your examples from the husband's perspective. When I read them, I completely agree and understand. However, I would not have come to that conclusion on my own." That this feels so foreign to women is a formidable barrier to success.

And sometimes, for the two of us, it can be a bit more than discouraging. We know the truth of what we are teaching, but convincing others can be a daunting task. I, Emerson, once wrote in my journal: "I am downcast. Lord, is it Your desire that I spend my remaining years trying to inform and convince women that they should feel excited about showing respect when women by nature do not 'feel' this way? They tell me again and again, 'This is so foreign.' They know it is true yet can't grasp it, and some don't want it to be true. My heart goes out to them. They are so tender, and can be so easily shamed. Yet, some can have a stubborn streak in them. Love is so consuming to them, which I applaud, that showing respect to a husband is not in their thought process. It seems so unnatural and uninviting. They apparently prefer not to go there. Some put their heels in. As one wife said, 'I am really resisting what is being said, but I know it is true, and I know I need to hear it.' They don't argue with me about it being untrue, they just go back to love. They go silent on this biblical injunction to show respect. As one wife told me, 'I want to love and be loved. I don't want to do this respect thing.' Lord, I thought this message would be a profound blessing but for some it is an unsought good. You know, Lord, I am not wired to 'sell' something that is unsought. I am not a marketer. I am up against something that isn't politically correct. Help me unfold Your Truth for them. May they look beyond their husbands and their negative feelings to Your Word in Ephesians 5:33b and 1 Peter 3:2. My confidence is Your Revelation. Please honor my feeble attempts to reduce divorce, reduce the number of children crying themselves to sleep, and bring about a measure of enjoyment in marriages. Help the wives see I am for them, not against them. Help them see You! In Your Name."

Arthur Schopenhauer (1788-1860) wrote, "All truth passes through three stages. First, it is ridiculed. Second, it is violently opposed. Third, it is accepted as being self-evident." I wish this weren't true about unconditional respect toward husbands, but we'll see. Are you ridiculing the idea? Are you furiously opposing it? Or is it self-evident?

Let us repeat, feelings are especially important to women. So if a wife doesn't feel that her husband deserves respect, she considers it somehow hypocritical and ridiculous for her to show him respect. You probably also don't feel like getting up when the alarm clock goes off, but you don't tell your friends, "I won't get up. It would be hypocritical. I don't feel like it, so I am not going to." Feelings can be irrelevant when acting responsibly. You don't want to fix your children's lunches or get up with them at night but you do. Your faith and values override your feelings. The same applies with unconditional respect. You do this as a demonstration of who you are, not because of who your husband is. You do this in response to Scripture regardless of feelings.

The Command God Did *Not* Give to Wives

Let's briefly review: no wife is commanded to love her husband with "agape" love, but both Paul and Peter do instruct unconditional respect. Paul, who penned 1 Corinthians 13, the love chapter, does not instruct a wife to agape-love her husband. Instead, he says, "respect her husband." Neither does Peter, who walked with the Lord of Love for three years, instruct a wife to agape-love her husband. He instructs that you can win him through your "respectful behavior."

When the Bible instructs in Titus 2:4, that the older women are to encourage the younger women to love their husbands and love their children, this is phileo-love or friendship love, not agape-love. Not "filet" him, but "phileo" him. A wife can become very unfriendly. Negativity can begin to control her as she tries to change her family, both husband and children. She agape-loves her family, but is very critical. She is no fun. There is too much anger. A husband can feel like the men in Esther, "the ladies...will speak in the same way...there will be plenty of contempt and anger" (Esther 1:18).

When the issue isn't the issue and you see your husband's spirit deflate and see him lose motivation to feel love for you, we predict he is feeling disrespected for who he is as a human being. We are not saying he is justified for these feelings. We are saying this is how he feels. This is why God is so clear in His commands in Ephesians 5:33b and 1 Peter 3:2. When a wife feels unloved she can react in ways at brief moments that are, frankly, uncivil. God knows this is counterproductive. It sends the wrong message to her husband. It does not accomplish what she hopes. Because she is so consumed with love she does not pay close enough attention to that sour reaction. Because the code is obvious to her, she assumes her husband should decode this. God knew blue hearing aids do not hear what pink hearing aids hear. The command is a megaphone to the wife: put on respect when feeling upset. God is saying that you can do this, and it is imperative that you do this for the sake of your relationship with Him, your husband and your children. If you hold onto the position that the problem is your husband and he needs to change, you cannot biblically justify that stance. Because he is called to love does not mean you can wait to show unconditional respect. God commands him to love. God commands you to respect. Your obedience is not contingent on his obedience. You cannot argue, "I'll respect after he loves."

Since Culture Advocates This Concept, Why Not God?

Some wives misunderstand the issues surrounding respect. They feel that by showing respect, they are tacitly buying into some idea that their husbands are superior to them. They feel this is a call to act as an inferior. In our culture, is this what we mean when teaching respect for all? Is the culture demanding we treat the other as a superior? "Now class, show respect toward Mary because she is superior to you." Is this what Aretha

Franklin wants – treatment as a supreme – when singing R.E.S.P.E.C.T.? God's Word is in no way saying a husband is higher. Peter precisely instructs husbands to view wives as "fellow heirs." Peter teaches wives to respect husbands in 1 Peter 3:2, but also announces husbands and wives are equal in God's eyes in 1 Peter 3:7. Five verses later! Those who think showing respect means paying homage to male superiority, have a contemporary cultural view. Peter clearly doesn't share that perspective.

Have you noticed that our culture advocates unconditional respect – except toward men and husbands? Respect is to be given regardless of race, gender, religion or sexual orientation. Husbands must merit this. In schools where respect for other people is taught as part of a tolerance philosophy, they are not saying others are superior. They are promoting equal treatment. The key is to respectfully disagree and disapprove. Showing respect does not mean we agree with the other's point of view or that we FEEL a flood of respect for the person. Respect means we show respect for who that person is in the Image of God. All people are created in the Image of God; therefore, it is okay to treat them with respect even though we go to our grave fighting against their cause. In fact, we can show respect toward a criminal who is awaiting a death sentence for crimes against our families. Respect does not mean removal of confrontation and consequences. Those in law enforcement show respect for their prisoners while handcuffing them. As Peter tells all believers, "honor all men." If damnation comes to a person, God does the damning. Disagreeing with your husband does not mean you have to be disrespectful. Feeling your husband is deserving of Hell does not mean you must manifest contempt. Scripture teaches, "Never take your own revenge, beloved, but leave room for the wrath of God, for it is written, 'Vengeance is Mine, I will repay,' says the Lord" (Romans 12:19). Some people have trouble showing respect when they feel the other's position or person is not worthy of respect. And if they don't respect what the person is doing, they feel justified for being dishonoring toward their person.

"What about a drunk husband, how can I

> "and those members of the body, which we deem less honorable, on these we bestow more abundant honor, and our unseemly members come to have more abundant seemliness."
> - I Corinthians 12:23

respect that?" Again, we are not talking about respecting the behavior, but about being a respectful person independent of another's failings. Why does one have to be disrespectful because one feels no respect? A husband may be a drunk in the gutter, but a wife can still show respect toward him as she brings the policeman to where he lies. As she grieves over the loss of love, she need not explode with vile words of disdain. She can be a woman of dignity though her husband lies in his vomit in an undignified manner. She can deem him less honorable yet bestow on him more abundant honor. Impossible? It is a biblical teaching (1 Corinthians 12:23). She would do it for her son if he was down and out. She would hope her daughter-in-law would do it toward her son.

The true measure of a wife – in God's eyes – is how she respectfully treats her husband who fails to love her as she dreams. Jesus said, "And if you love those who love you, what credit is that to you? For even sinners love those who love them" (Luke 6:32). To love a husband God's way is to show unconditional respect at the point of conflict.

Critics of this message will say we are subjecting women to physical abuse. Our answer again is, "Absolutely not!" We recognize evil. We preach against evil far more than most. We respond when Forrest Gump watches his female friend deal with her childhood sexual abuse. As she revisits the home where the abuse happened, she picks up rocks and starts throwing them at the house. Forrest says, "Sometimes there just aren't enough rocks." Our hearts break at that. As for abuse, Paul himself encourages a wife to separate from her husband under certain circumstances (1 Corinthians 7:11). No doubt Paul had abuse in mind. Scripture condemns such atrocities (Jude 19:25). When there is life-threatening abuse, a wife should separate immediately. She must turn to people who can intervene (Romans 13:4). No wife is to remain in harm's way. We have zero tolerance for such evil behavior. However, the word abuse is too loosely thrown around.

This bears repeating. Some women exclaim, "He is so abusive! He doesn't talk to me." That hardly qualifies as persecution. Some use the phrase "he's abusive," and become convinced that is the case. If a wife is trying to transform her good-willed husband by saying this though she knows it isn't true, it won't motivate him to be more talkative. If she believes he is abusive when he is not, it will not motivate him to have fond feelings of love for her. And, as we've made the case, he may be seeking to do the honorable thing by going quiet during conflict. We believe numerous wives have missed the hearts of their husbands in a colossal way. We received a note from a widow friend. She wrote, "I know a woman who made a choice to respect her husband and to be his friend when others considered him repulsive and despicable because of ongoing alcoholism. She stood by him and even demanded her children respect their father because he was their father. Her continual prayer was that her husband would come to know the Lord. I'm sure she deferred because she continued to remain even when he was abusive and drunk. She cooked meals when he arrived home late, often in the middle of the night. She didn't badger him, but continued to use a kind and gentle spirit. She became a servant, cleaning up vomit following bouts of drunkenness. He finally became seriously ill and allowed her to read the Bible to him each day and pray. She finally led him to the Lord. He died some time later, but rejoicing because of his salvation. You may ask, 'Should any woman have to sacrifice a whole life for such a person?' Our answer is the sacrifice wasn't only for a drunken man, but for her wonderful family of five children. Four out of five are in the ministry; one is a pastor, one teaches at Stonybrook, one teaches music at HCJB, and a daughter is on the mission field. The children and husband watched the life of this woman, unappreciated, abused and neglected – and they saw love instead of nagging, retaliation or vindictiveness – and they learned to love the Lord she loved."

Should that wife have stayed in the marriage? We were unclear about the word "abusive." When we read that word, we assumed it was verbal abuse. Had it been physical, we could not endorse what this woman did. Given it was verbal abuse – as rotten as that is – the man had an addiction. It wasn't "for better" but "for worse." No doubt, this wife would say it was worth sticking out even in the face of emotional abuse. She was an example of authenticity. The primary critics of this do not see God and His plan; they do not have an eternal perspective. Such emotional suffering makes no sense to them. For this wife, throughout eternity, she will know it was worth it. It was worth it as her adult children stood around her casket speaking of her as the most loving and respectful human being they knew and then carrying on her faith after she's gone. It was worth it.

What this story highlights for us is the contrast with some wives today. Because their emotional needs are not being met to the level they expect, they label their husbands as abusive and divorce them. The truth is few husbands are in the gutter or physically abusive; most wives are married to good-willed men. How sad that contempt is shown toward good men– so good they entrust their children to their care! But divorces happen, for no other reason than these men aren't who women want them to be.

Is Self-Examination Good for the Soul?

Work with us. We need to say something painful. A wife may be disrespectful because she is like one "who has no control over his spirit" (Proverbs 25:28). She is an accident waiting to happen. She is an angry soul, and

> "She eats and wipes her mouth, And says, 'I have done no wrong.'"
> - Proverbs 30:20

her husband happens to be in her sights (Proverbs 21:19). Unwilling to acknowledge this, she denounces the idea of showing respect. In order to justify her lack of self-control and resentment, she blames her husband. The appeal we make is to allow God to encourage her and see the bigger picture. If she is not honest with herself, she will quench love in her marriage. Feeling and showing disrespect for who he is as a man will not motivate him to feel and show love for

> "...quench love..."
> - Solomon 8:7

> "She is boisterous and rebellious."
> - Proverbs 7:11

her. This is especially so if he is an innocent person.

Think about the following. During the break at a marriage conference, Zack says to Suzy, "Wasn't that so true? 'A gal marries a guy thinking she'll love him into change. A guy marries thinking the gal will never change. Then, after marriage she says, 'He'll never change!' He says, 'That's not the gal I married.' Wow. How true. Wasn't that funny?" Suzy says, "That's right. But it's not funny. I have tried to love you every which way but you *never* change. To be honest with you, that's why I feel so little respect for you right now. I don't want to hurt your feelings, but that's how I feel." Zack deflates. He hardly says anything the rest of the conference. He takes no more notes. Mentally, he is miles away. Suzy feels bad about what she said. That, though, is how she feels, and he needs to deal with her feelings. (What if he said, "I don't want to hurt your feelings, but I don't love you"?)

The feelings of a wife tend to dominate the marital scene. A wife wants her feelings validated. But we need to step back; not all feelings are valid. How can a wife justify contempt in direct disobedience to God's Word? Without question, God is calling each wife to trust His Word above the senses.

> "for we walk by faith, not by sight..."
> - 2 Corinthians 5:7

Billy is a pig farmer. He never went to college. Ann married Billy because of his kindness, integrity, and faith. But after fifteen years and three children, Ann wanted something more. Billy was no match to the romance novels. Billy was not selfish. When he had extra, he gave it to her. Even so, she had become critical of farm life and of Billy. He smelled. She decided to go to college. He got extra pigs to pay for it. After a year, she surfaced with the idea of divorce. Billy couldn't eat for a week. He wanted them to get counseling. Ann would only see a professor of women's studies. As Billy sat there listening to this professor talk about a woman's needs, and

> "Let marriage be held in honor among all, and let the marriage bed be undefiled; for fornicators and adulterers God will judge." - Hebrews 13:4

that Ann needed more than Billy could give, Billy said, "Ma'am. I know I'm not much. I'm a pig farmer. But I've always loved Ann. I'd die for her. You have to make a commitment. 'Til death do us part." The professor said, "Billy, you're a good man but being an uneducated farmer, you just don't understand how to bring romance into a woman's life." Ann divorced him. She wanted to feel love, to feel alive. Something died in Billy. Sometimes late at night in the pig barn he'd cry, saying to himself, "I ain't nothing but a pig myself. I'm a nobody."

A Husband's Feelings

Your husband is as sensitive to certain symbols – things that cause him to feel you do not respect him – as you are sensitive to symbols that he may not love you. For example, during the Christmas season, a wife shared with her husband that many of the neighbor la- **"she wept before him** dies went to a large city to shop. She said, "Can **seven days...And it** you believe they're going to all those expensive **came about on the** stores?" She continued on but noticed her hus- **seventh day that he** band going quiet, and then the rest of the evening **told her because she pressed him hard."** he was withdrawn and in a bad mood. Later she — Judges 14:17 discovered that he felt she was sending him a message. He thought her code was, "You aren't making enough. You're less successful. You can't provide what I want. I don't respect you like I respect the husbands who can provide more for their wives. You're a loser."

She was stunned. She was making conversation. Unlike most women, men tend to feel their hurts and then put them into compartments. Men are far less expressive about their inner feelings. A major reason is that when men feel disrespected, they feel too vulnerable sharing those feelings. Being disrespected is a gigantic pain in their hearts. They fear surfacing that feeling. She might dismiss his feelings as childish, or worse, she'll reiterate that she does not respect him. She has been given full rights to say, "I don't respect you." When it comes to marriage today, the feelings of some wives serve as the criteria for what is legitimate. So, if she is upset over her body-image, that is valid. If she is depressed over her failings as a mother, especially if he suggests she is way too negative, her depression is valid. But, if he goes quiet over a disrespectful comment she makes at a PMS moment, not only is he wrong for going silent, he should be loving enough to empathize with her frustrations and attack. The present cultural teaching is that husbands need to understand. If though, he is hurt by her suggestion that he isn't making enough money, but she meant no harm, he is childish for sulking over the feeling of being dishonored. "Men are so self-centered!" She then wonders why he doesn't talk to her that evening.

Affecting Your Husband's Feelings: Igniting Fond Feelings of Love

You don't have to live this way. You don't have to remain in ignorance, being darkened in your understanding. God's Light has been given to you! You can motivate him to respond in new and meaningful ways. Faith in God's Word will guide you. You have discovered the one word

> "walk no longer just as the Gentiles also walk...being darkened in their understanding...because of the ignorance that is in them."
>
> - Ephesians 4:17, 18

that motivates your husband more than any other word. You have discovered and believed what the Bible declares. **Now you're ready to move from the discovery to the application.** In book two, we'll get very practical. We'll help you apply the one word that energizes your husband to love. We believe you can increase his feelings of love for you. We believe he will be more expressive and responsive than before. Let's move forward. Let's get concrete answers to the most critical question of all: **What can a wife specifically do that motivates her husband God's way?**

If you do not have book two, Motivating Your Man God's Way: Applying One Word that Motivates Your Husband to Love, it's available at: www.loveandrespect.com.

Publications referenced throughout text:

Berry, Jo. 1983. *Beloved Unbeliever: Loving Your Husband into the Faith.* Grand Rapids: Zondervan.

Dobson, James. 1997. *Solid Answers.* Carol Stream, Ill: Tyndale House Publishers.

Gottman, John, and Silver, Nan. 1994. *Why Marriages Succeed or Fail: And How You Can Make Yours Last.* New York: Simon & Schuster Publishers.